LONDON BORN

LONDON BORN

SIDNEY DAY

Compiled and edited by Helen Day

FOURTH ESTATE • *London*

First published in Great Britain in 2004 by
Old Git Publications
This edition published by Fourth Estate
An imprint of HarperCollins*Publishers*
77–85 Fulham Palace Road
London W6 8JB

1

A catalogue record for this book is
available from the British Library

ISBN 0–00–720384–5

Typeset in Meridien by
Rowland Phototypesetting Ltd, Bury St Edmunds, Suffolk

Printed in Great Britain by Clays Ltd, St Ives plc

PART ONE

I

'Sid . . . Sid!' Me mother was calling for me. I'm not kidding you – if there was five hundred people lived in our street, there was five hundred people out on the road, all looking at me. Me mum and a policeman was standing outside our house. Next to them was Mrs Leicester from the shop down the road. I thought about running but they had already seen me.

Me mum says, 'You've had a loaf out of her shop and she wants the fourpence ha'penny for it.'

'Pay up, you saucy sod,' says Mrs Leicester.

She had come to find me. I don't know how she knew it was me stole the bread, but there she was outside our house. I held out tuppence ha'penny. Me mum clumped me round the ear'ole.

'Get inside!'

The policeman come inside with us. Me mum told him she had given me some money that morning and sent me to get a loaf of bread from Leicester's shop.

I says, 'Mrs Leicester weren't about so I took it.'

I had crept in, picked up a nice crusty cottage loaf and slid out. After I got it home I thought to meself, 'That's fourpence

ha'penny I've saved there.' So I went up to the faggot shop
on the corner of our road and spent tuppence on faggot and
pease pudding – two lots on a piece of newspaper.

'I ought to nick you,' the policeman says.

But he just gave me a rollicking and it all got washed over
at the death. All I got was a bleeding good hiding from me
mum. Then she locked me in the bedroom. I was in there for
hours. It got late and I could hear them all down in the
kitchen. On the next floor up lived Wiggy Lenny. I went to
the window and opened it.

I says, 'Wig!'

After two or three times he opened the window.

'What do you want?'

'Got anything to eat? I ain't had nothing.'

'I got some melon I nicked.'

'Give us a bit then – I'm bleeding starving.'

He tied the melon on a piece of string and dangled it down.
Just as I grabbed it me mum come in and didn't she smack
me arse.

Me mum never let me get away with anything. She would
say, 'Don't you ever do that again,' and then – bang! She
gave me some whackings but it only made me worse. The
old man was away in the war and so me mum gave the
orders. Sometimes, if the old man was home on leave and
we made him really angry, he would unthread his Army
belt, raise it up and roar at us – but he never hit us. It was
me mum who would wring our necks if she found us out.
Luckily, she never really knew what we was up to. Every day
I nicked something from the shops and stalls round Archway,
specially the greengrocer's. If you are hungry you got to live.

They called me mum Dinah Day, but I think her real name
was Alice Maud. Dad was William Day. We lived in Balmore
Street, N19, a street where there was so much villainry going

on, so many drunks and gambling and Gawd knows what, that at night the police would only come down in twos. Everyone knew it as Tiger Bay.

The house we lived in had two floors and a basement. The Lennys had the top floor and we had the first floor and the airy below. There was Mum, Dad, Alice, Bill, Bob, Jim, me and Lulu. On the pavement outside there was a round hole with a lid that was once the coal hole for the cellar. Me mate, Bill Rudd, who we called Ruddy, slept in the cellar on a mattress that me mum slung down there for him.

Ruddy's real home was further up the street, four houses past the alley that went down to our school. Before he come to us his mum died and he lived for a while with his sister and his old man. His dad was a very strict old boy – a 'stiff collar' sort who liked a drink but never got drunk. He was a grave digger for donkey's years at Highgate Cemetery, but he earned poor money – very poor money. Ruddy's sister was a nurse up the hospital. Ruddy come to live with us when she found a bloke and moved out. Every day me mum gave me a cup of tea and a slice of bread and dripping to take down to him. The rest of his food he had to find hisself.

Our garden was just like all the other gardens in the street. We had one toilet for the two families and there was always a row about who should clean it out. The rest of the garden was filled with me dad's geraniums, and pens and sheds for our chickens, ducks and rabbits. We kept pigeons to race and had an aviary full of wild birds. Our dogs was kept out there too – everyone in the street had dogs.

When I was only about four years old I went into the garden and seen one of our teeny chicks dragging his leg.

I says to me brother, 'Oh look, Bill, that poor chicken has broke his leg.'

'Has it?'

'Yeah, poor thing.'

Bill says, 'Go along to the chemist shop and get him some sixpenny chicken crutches.'

He gave me a sixpence and I went into the chemist at the end of our street. Inside was Mr Armitage, the tall old boy what owned it.

I says, 'Can I have a pair of sixpenny crutches for me chicken?'

Didn't he laugh! When I got home Bill thought it was a great joke.

At the other end of our street a family called the Booths had a greengrocer's shop. There was nineteen kids in that family and me mum was midwife to the lot. She brought all of them into the world. Cor blimey, what a family! Old Mother Booth was a fat woman with great big breasts, and she was the boss alright. Mr Booth was only a little old boy, no more than five foot high. He maintained Highgate Cemetery and moved big tombstones onto the graves from the stonemason's next door. His poor old horse, Nobby, had to move them stones round all bleeding day. We called him Rat-tailed Nobby cause he only had a little tail.

The cemetery was right next to our street, so me and me mates was always larking round in there. On Sundays it was filled with dozens of people come to visit graves. It was a long walk from some of the graves to the water tap. We sold clean jam jars to the mourners for a penny each and filled them up with water for a penny more. When they had gone we pinched the flowers off the graves and sold them. We took the wreaths too, pulled the moss off and sold them for a ha'penny back to the florist.

II

I was five years old when I started school, the year before the fourteen war ended. The sky was filled with observation balloons. There was two blokes sat inside each basket looking for German aircraft coming in. We waved at them from the school playground and they waved back at us. The balloons was up there night and day, hundreds of them, all over the show.

The war never really meant anything to us kids. Me mum would put a blanket all the way round our big table in the kitchen and say, 'Get under there.' That table was our air raid shelter. We all got tucked in underneath and thought it was a bit of fun. The Booths would come over to our house and get under the table or under the stairs with us. Sometimes me gran was there too.

Me gran was always in and out of our house or me mum would go up the road to her house. We always shouted out when we passed her sitting on her step. Sometimes she would send me for a jug of black beer and I would drink a drop on the way back. She was a little old Spanish woman with a long black plait down her back. I don't think I knew her name – we just called her Gran. She was always in black. Her skirt was tight round her waist and it come out down to the floor. She looked like a little tent walking round. Lots of women wore those long dresses dragging the ground and they got filthy at the bottom. Me gran was a nice old lady. Mind you, if you was cheeky to her she slapped you round the ear'ole – bang! – no arguments. She was very strict.

When the war started hotting up we all traipsed down

to the tube station and slept on the platform every night. Everybody in the street went down there. Cor blimey, it stunk like merry hell with all the drunken old sods, stunk terrible. The only good thing about it was it was nice and warm. When they knew there was going to be an air raid the fire engine went along the top of the road sounding the sirens. It was a cart with a big tank in the middle and a big pump on it, drawn by horses. When they blew the old bugle you knew there was an air raid coming. Once I seen a fleet of German airplanes come low across over our house, flying in the shape of a tick.

There weren't a lot of bombing but I can remember four bombs. The very first one hit Highgate Hospital. It landed right on the big iron gates. The gatekeeper weren't there so nobody got killed – it just blew the gates away. The next one was at the foot of Parliament Hill Fields as you enter from West Hill. We used that one as a swimming pool when it got full up with water. Another fell not far from the Highgate ponds.

The fourth bomb was dropped near the gun on the top of Parliament Hill. It practically landed on me Uncle Fred who ran a gun called Big Bertha. A little dog, a whippet, ran into the fenced off area round the gun during that air raid. Nobody claimed it so me uncle bought it down to our house. He would often come over with some food for us. You could walk it in a quarter of an hour.

Me mum says to him, 'Ooo he's a lovely little boy, ain't he?'

He says, 'It ain't a boy it's a gel. Do you want her?'

'Yeah, I'll have her, lovely little dog.'

'Alright, Dinah. Take her on.'

So we got the dog. Mum called her Nel and kept her for fourteen years. She was me mother's water bottle. She used to get into the bed and wiggle her way down to the bottom and the old gel would put her feet on her of a night time.

We always had two or three dogs living with us. I had a Bull Terrier, but I don't know if I ever give him a name. I had him a couple or three years but then he strangled hisself with his tether in the garden. We had another little dog, a black and white Jack Russell, and he could pick a penny up off the floor when you threw it down for him. That wants some doing for a dog. Me favourite dog was called Babs. She was an Airedale with a lovely brown and black coat, all tight curls, a lovely dog. Sometimes I took three dogs out at a time over Parliament Hill Fields. In the war it was a training ground for the Army. I seen many two-wheel gun carriages tip arse over head there. They come flying down the hill pulled by four horses, as fast as they could go. When the carriage tipped over the soldiers would put it back on its wheels and off they would go again, round and round.

All the men was away in the war. Me dad was in the Army. He served the whole length of the war in the Royal Artillery, driving the horses that pulled the guns. That was how he got the name Driver Day. He was short and well built with brown hair and he was covered all over with tattoos. His nose was spread across his chops from fighting. When he had leave from the Army he would come home, straight out of the trenches, mud everywhere, filthy. The poor old bugger had puttees wrapped round his legs up to his knees and the mud was all caked in where they hadn't been taken off for weeks and weeks. His legs looked like ladders from the marks round them made by the ties.

When me mum said Dad was coming home, Jim and me would wait for him at the top of our road. He was always glad to see us. He brought these great big dog biscuits for us called 'iron rations' and we liked to eat them. Mind you, they was only nice cause we had nothing else. You had to have a hammer to break the bleeding things.

Me dad was out in the front line for years in France. He was fit as a fiddle and a keen old fighter. When it was peaceful they put up boxing rings and he would organise boxing exhibitions. He was popular – anybody who done a lot of sport in the Army always got on. As well as boxing they larked about in the trenches, gambling for cigarettes, and sometimes, he told me, they would go into farms, nick a pig, take it back to the trenches and roast it. When a horse got shot in battle, as soon as it was down and out, they would carve it up with their bayonets and eat that as well.

While me dad was away, me mum had to keep the seven of us on rations. I would go round and get food from Buckingham's shop. Mum would say, 'Take the cup with you and get an haporth of jam, a pennorth of sugar, a bit of tea, a tin of evaporated milk and a lump of margarine.' We hardly ever see any meat.

III

The war ended and me dad come home. After he got gassed in France he never could breathe through his nose properly again. Sometimes he was in so much pain with his nose he would come home from work at dinner time and put his head over a bowl of hot salt water and sniff it up. That was the only way he could shift it.

Me mum's brother, Bob, who lived right opposite us, was much worse off. He lived with his wife Ginny and their kids. He was a typical looking Spanish man if ever there was one

– sharp featured and sticking out black hair. His face always looked black from wanting a shave, what was left of it. He had half his jaw blown off in the war. For a pension he got the big amount of two and sixpence a week. The poor old bugger only had half a jaw and looked a sight but he got used to it at the death. He still knew how to drink a pint of beer.

The men went back to work, if they could find work. On every street corner there was gangs of men chinwagging cause they didn't have the money to go for a pint. It was hard to get a proper job and that was why so many young blokes from our street joined the Army, even after the war. They sent them out to India after they was trained. I think there was a place called Tiger Bay out there and that is how our street come to get its name.

The winter after me dad come home he got the job of night watchman on the other side of the cemetery where they was putting in some drainage. On his first night me mum sent me up with some food. Dad told me to cut through the cemetery on the way back. I had to walk past the gravestones and stone angels glowing all white in the dark. I did that every night while he was up there and I never told him I was afraid.

Me dad worked mainly in the building. After a day's work he was always in the pub. He lived there. He loved his pint, they all did. That was all they had to do, let's face it – drink and make babies. Our two local pubs was called the Totnes and the Brookfield – they was only a few minutes apart. Each of them had two bars and an off licence. One bar was for the navvies, the hard workers, and the other for the shopkeepers and people who had a bob or two. They called that the saloon bar and you had to pay extra for yer booze in there. It was a bit more upmarket, with chairs, tables and flowers. There was a brass rail running along the counter and red velvet curtains hanging round to make it look pretty. The navvies' bar had big benches, sawdust on the floor and spittoons along the counter.

The pubs opened at five o'clock and kicked out at ten o'clock on the dot unless they had the Law straightened up. The guvnor at the Brookfield always took out a pint of beer to a policeman who drunk it in the outside toilet. Saturday nights there would be hollering and shouting and fighting and blokes up to all manner of things. That was how it was. If you fell out with a bloke you stood up and had a fight. When it was over you was back friends again. Some of them went singing in the streets. They would come down our road from the pub, half drunk, get a comb out and a piece of paper and play a tune and people would give them a ha'penny or a penny. One bloke would put his foot in the door, stand there and sing his heart out and then take his hat inside for pennies.

The next day they was back in the pub. The Irish blokes would go up to St Joseph's, 'Holy Joe's', at the top of Dartmouth Park Hill. They would confess and give the priest a shilling. Then they would hare down to the Archway Tavern. A while later the priest would go down there too, taking off his dog collar as he walked along and putting a handkerchief round his neck. He would go in, spend all their money and they would all wind up drunk as lords.

On a Sunday morning our road was full up with ponies pulling gigs, come to race. The gigs was painted in bright blues and reds and the ponies had lovely shiny coats. They was all done up with ribbons and bows – a picture to look at. People come from all round to watch them fly up and down and they would bet on all types of things – whose pony would win, whose pony was done up best. The old ponies would prance up and down the street, lifting their hooves up high. They trained them to do that by tying a rope between the pony's legs and the bridle. As the pony's head come up his hooves had to follow. After the races and the betting all the ponies and chariots would be tied up outside the pub.

Nearly everybody who went to the Brookfield on a Sunday took a bird in a little carrying cage. Me dad took his cage wrapped up in a red and white spotted navvy's handkerchief so his bird wouldn't be afraid. He would put the cage underneath his arm and take off the cloth when he got to the pub. Every man put his bird up on the shelf that ran right the way along the bar. The bar was filled with birds fluttering and singing.

Me dad had dozens of different birds: finches, linnets, thrushes, blackbirds. There weren't a type of bird that breathed that me dad didn't have at some time. We caught them by going bush bashing. Me dad made eight foot by three foot double-layered nets out of black cotton. We would loop a net between two trees in Kenwood and then bash the bushes with sticks to scare the birds towards it. When a bird flew through the net it was trapped in a pocket.

I went bird nesting and egg collecting with me brothers, too. We collected eggs, made two holes in them with a pin and blew them empty. Sometimes we took birds when they was near to being fledged. I reared them up, feeding them chewed up bread from me mouth or on a matchstick. I brought up lots of birds, including a sparrowhawk. It was a very pretty bird with zebra markings and I let it go at the finish.

In the pub they bet on the birds. One might say, 'Me bird will sing longer than yours.' Another might boast, 'Mine will sing better than yours,' and another, 'Me bird's plumage is better than yours.' Then they would have a competition. That bird in its little cage was their pride and joy. Everybody had birds, everybody.

When the Brookfield kicked out after lunch me dad would walk home with his bird. As he turned into the Bay he would stop outside the house of Drummer Hawkins who lived at the top of our road. 'Hawkins,' he would shout, 'come out here, I'll see to yer!' Hawkins was twice me dad's size, a brute of a man. When he heard me dad hollering he would come out and they would whip off their shirts and fight like tigers. There would be blood and snot everywhere. Me dad loved a good fight. That evening they would be drinking together in the pub.

The pubs was always full up with hounds gambling. Me brother Bill worked as runner to a penny bookmaker. He collected the bets and took them in. Sometimes the police would come into the pub and he had to give them five bob beer money. The police looked forward to it – that's all they went in for, to cop their money off of the bookmakers or the gamblers. On one occasion two plainclothes policemen – two real bastards – come into the Brookfield.

They says to me brother, 'Come on, cough up.'

He emptied his pockets and they went out and round to the saloon bar. Then in come the Inspector and nicked Bill just the same. He got a thirty bob fine.

The elder ones in the Bay was mostly always drunk. They liked a pint of black beer – the cheapest beer you could buy. A pint of black was five pence and other beer was sixpence a pint. The old biddies liked a drop of biddy wine. It was wine from the bottom of the barrel and it was thick like mud. The old gels would take their bottles into the pub and get three pennorth of it. It was the cheapest form of drink to get drunk on quick – it would blow yer hat off. It was also the favourite drink of worn-out prostitutes. Nearly everyone liked a drop to drink, and plenty drank theirselves to death.

When someone died in our street the family would go

in the pub with the collection. They wore black armbands. Everyone would throw in a few coppers, thruppence, six-pence – or whatever – for the family. Most people had a parish funeral cause their families couldn't afford to pay for a proper one. A proper funeral cost six pounds and it was a big event, everybody turned out. They paraded the coffin through the streets covered in flowers. The glass-sided hearse was pulled by black horses with beautiful plumes sticking right up. They was stabled at the top of our street. The horses' hooves would be muffled by straw put on the road to stop the noise and everyone would come outside and watch them go by.

Me gran died when I was still very young. I don't remember her having a funeral but she must have done. The day she died me mum was sitting down with me sisters when I come indoors.

'Yer granny's dead,' she says.

'Well it won't burn yer lips to kiss her arse then, will it!' I says, quick as anything.

It just come out. Didn't she give me a tanning. I was the youngest son and a bit of a favourite with me mum, but that time I think I really upset her. I suppose I thought nothing of death then. People was always dying or getting born.

IV

Everybody thought the world of me mum. Everybody in the Bay who had children, me mum brought them into the world. I don't know what people said about the rest of us cause we was always up to villainry, always. But compared

to the others in the street we was pretty prim and proper,
our family. We wasn't dirty and scruffy. Oh blimey, some
never washed for bleeding weeks in the Bay.

Me mum always wore a black dress with a potato sack
taped round her as an apron. She was always cooking or
round the wash pot. She worked from about six in the morning till she went to bed, doing housework and washing and
ironing. She did all the washing for the Booths as well as
bringing them into the world. More or less anything wanted
doing it was, 'Go and see Dinah, she'll do it.'

She would stand for hours at the copper in the scullery
with a big white bar of Lifebuoy soap, rubbing and squeez-
ing the clothes. We helped her by keeping the old copper
going. We chopped wood to feed the fire and sometimes we
burned old lino. The copper used to boil lovely when you
put that on. Lots of houses had green or red lino made of
tar, and it was thrown out when it got too cracked. When
somebody burned lino the smoke outside was thick and
black.

We took turns putting the clean clothes and linen through
the old iron wringer. Then Mum emptied the copper of
all the water. At Christmas time we boiled the ham and
the potatoes in that copper cause there was so many of
us to feed. Every year me mum also used it to steam eight
Christmas puddings and we usually ate the last one at
Easter.

Me mum was the pawn shop runner for the whole street.
She got so much in the shilling off people to take their stuff
to and from the pawn shop, or 'Uncle Bill's' as all pawn shops
was known. All of us was in the same boat as far as money
was concerned. Two pound twelve and sixpence a week was
an average wage. We had to pay everything out of that –
food, clothing and health insurance. In the building game

there was no such thing as a regular job. The money never lasted the week so most families got by with the help of the pawn shop.

'Uncle Bill' took in people's valuables and clothes and charged a penny in the shilling when they bought them back. Every Monday morning me mum would do up her hair in earmuffs, put on her bonnet, tie the ribbons underneath and get out the old Bassinette pram. She would take me dad's waistcoat and war medals, put them in the pram, and set off for the pawn shop on the corner of Tufnell Park, by the tube.

As she went along the street people hollered out to her, 'Take this for me Day-o,' and she would pile everything into the pram. She took it in Monday, pawned it for the week, and then brought it back on Saturday. Going down Dartmouth Park Hill on a Monday with all the stuff was alright, but coming back up on a Saturday was a push – it was terrible. The pram was loaded right up high with parcels and it near took her all bleeding day.

We took it in turns to go with Mum to the pawn shop and help her push the pram. We would pass lots of other people on the streets, and cattle, pigs and flocks of sheep on their way to London Caledonian Market.

When we got to the shop she would go into a cubicle. The shop was divided into cubicles so nobody could see what you had to pawn. We stood and waited for 'Uncle Bill' to fill out the tickets. Then it was home, back up that hill. Me poor mum, what with that and all the washing, ironing and cooking, she was worn out before she died, poor old sod.

V

I got up every morning before six o'clock when me dad hollered up the stairs, 'Get out of kip!' I had a cold water wash in the washhouse, scrubbed meself with carbolic soap and then had a cup of tea. I might do the bread run – nine times out of ten we bought stale bread. Me mum would give me her pillowcase and I would take it up to the shop and get it filled for sixpence. When I got back I would have some bread – and jam too, if I could. Then I would get Ruddy out of the coal cellar or find one of me other mates.

There was always people in the street, even early in the morning, sitting on their steps like blackbirds. It was good to get outside and away from the bugs indoors. The bugs was constantly eating away the mortar and the wood. A lot of houses never had wallpaper, only matchboarding painted with green or white limewash. Millions of bugs lived behind that matchboard. Sometimes when me and me brother Jim spotted them we would pick one each going up the wall and have a race. Me mum was always buying stuff to put round the iron bed to try and get rid of them. They sucked yer blood, they would bite terrible and they stank when you squashed them.

One morning, early, I met up with Joey Booth, the youngest of the Booth boys, who was the same age as me. He was pulling our four-wheel cart. It had a plank of wood for a swivel axle, two big pram wheels at the back and two smaller wheels at the front. A lump of rope was the steering wheel.

'Let's take the cart out before we have to go to school, Cabby,' he says.

'Alright,' I says.

Everyone called me Cabby cause I spent a lot of time outside the station carrying people's bags to the cabs for a few pennies. As soon as I see a woman come out with some big cases I would run up and say, 'Do you want a cab, ma'am?' and she would say, 'Yes, please.' Then I would take the cases over to the cab rank in the middle of St John's Road.

Joey and I took turns on the cart: one of us pushed while the other drove. Eventually we got to Dartmouth Park Hill. We spotted a baker's barrow standing on its own. The bloke was down the hill with his basket delivering bread and cakes door to door. We waited till he weren't looking and crept over to the barrow. There was racks of little loaves and cakes inside and tucked in a corner was a money pouch. Joey reached in and took sixpence out.

It turned out that the bloke always left his barrow there cause he didn't want to push it back up the hill. So every morning for months and months we took sixpence out of his pouch. There was probably thirty bob in there altogether, but we never took a lot out and he never noticed it was gone. That was a game, that was! We would spend the sixpence on food on our way to school.

When we wasn't at school we was always outside doing jobs, scrounging or playing in the street. We was never indoors. There was always a big gang of kids playing games in our street. We would line up some screws and aim cherry pips at them to see how many each of us could win – that was called cherry hogging. We would play hopscotch and spinning tops and race each other. We would throw a rope over the arm of a lamppost and swing round and round on it. If it was a summer evening and me dad was sitting on the steps outside our house he might say, 'There's a ha'penny for the first one round the block,' and we would tear off. Sometimes we played a game called 'Release'. We would chalk a big box on the street and then split into two teams. One side went and hid and the other team had to find them, one by one, and put them in the box. At any time their mates, if it was all clear, could run to the box and holler out 'Release!' to free the blokes in the box. We played lots of other games too, but nine times out of ten it was fighting.

Me dad taught me how to fight in the back garden. 'Cabby Day from Tiger Bay,' he would sing as he hopped about. 'The only man to go fifteen rounds with a wasp and never get stung!' We liked to have street fights with other streets. Our street would go round to Chesnall Road and fight a gang round there. There was the Tiger Bay mob, Raydon Street mob, Doighton Street mob and Dartmouth Hill mob. Each road had its own little mob of hounds. Sometimes we went over to Campbell Bunk in Lower Holloway where me uncle, Tinker Day, lived. It was the worst place in the country I should think; the most violent road there ever was for drunks, prostitution – you name it, it all happened in Campbell Bunk. They burned the floorboards, the joists, the doors – burned everything to keep warm – and nobody dared go near them to ask for any rent. Me own uncle was pretty bad when it come down to it, though I never had much to do with him or me cousins really, apart from going to fight them occasionally with the mob from our street.

When we wasn't fighting we might try tormenting the old people in the Bay. For our favourite trick we needed a reel of black cotton, a button and a pin. When it was dark we would dig the pin in the putty over the top of a window. Then we tied the button on the cotton and dangled it over. We took the reel across the road and tugged it so that the button kept on tapping on the window of the house, 'pip,

pip'. They would come out, look round and say, 'What the bleeding hell's happening here?' We drove the poor old sods mad with that. They was always telling us off, throwing a bucket of water over us and Gawd knows what else. 'Sling yer hook out of it,' they would say, and we would go back to our other games.

There was seasons for the different types of games like cherry hogging and top spinning. We would go from one game to another. There was special times in the year for other things too, like Guy Fawkes. We looked forward to that most of all. Each year we made a guy out of potato sacks stuffed with straw and gave it a mask for a face. Me mother sewed on the arms and the legs for us and we took the guy round the streets in a barrow hollering, 'Penny for the guy, penny for the guy!' The best places to go was outside the big hotels. One year we got more than eight shillings in a day doing that. We spent the money on sweets and fireworks for the big bonfire that was lit every year in the middle of our street.

We thought up some other ways to get hold of money, too. Opposite Buckingham's in Raydon Street there was an off licence run by a woman. All the empty bottles was kept in the side garden in Doighton Street where the lorries loaded and unloaded. I was passing one day with Ruddy and Joey Booth when I had an idea.

I says, 'Give me a hoof up.'

Ruddy shot me up and over the green doors of the gate. Soon I climbed back with some empty bottles.

'What are you going to do with them?' says Joey.

'Wait here a minute.'

I took the empties into the shop and got tuppence a bottle. After that we was over those bleeding doors all the time. One day the woman in the shop took a long look at me.

She says, 'Where d'you keep getting all these bottles from?'
I says, 'Over the hill.'
'Over the hill?'
I says, 'Yeah.'
She says, 'They must do a lot of drinking over there.'

She never did find us out. Daytime, night time, any bleed-ing time we passed, we would go and get three or four of her own bottles to return to her.

Another time I went into the coal and greengrocer's shop round the corner in Raydon Street. I crept along, bent down under the window and went through the door. Me mates waited outside. I couldn't see the owner, Mrs Stevens, so I took a handful of peanuts. Just as I passed the board that divided the vegetables from the coal she sprung out and caught me. She hit me so hard with her broom she knocked me scrabbling into the coal. Then she chased me round and round, over the heap of coal, hitting me all the time till I got out. Me mates was laughing so much they could hardly run. All that for a few bleeding peanuts!

VI

Alice was the eldest of us kids. She had long black hair right down her back and she was a greedy cow. She would sit cracking nuts by the fire and not give you a shell. I didn't live with her for long cause she went into service when she was fifteen and then got married and moved to the other end of the street.

Bill was the oldest boy. He was smart and good looking with tight curly hair and he was always joking. He worked in the building with me dad and sometimes gave me a penny to spend. Bob was next – he was the quiet one. He looked the most Spanish and his hair was wavy and as black as coal. He had eyes like a hawk – he could kill a bird with a single stone – and he wound up a champion darts player. He liked to walk over Hampstead Heath three or four times a day with his friend George Mead. George was long, like all his family, and he wound up about six foot seven. He had a lurcher that would tear other dogs to bits. He and Bob would set their dogs to fight other dogs up on the heath.

Me brother Jim was closest to me in age and we spent a lot of time together with Ruddy and our other mates. Lulu was the youngest and she was all up front. She was a spitfire and we was always fighting. Once I hit her round the ear'ole and she flew up the stairs after me and stabbed me in the arse with a pair of scissors. She always wanted me to give her money. I was one for saving and I always had a few coppers in me pocket. I don't think she liked it cause gels couldn't go scrounging and scrumping like boys could.

Like me brothers, I always wore a cap and I had no hair. Me dad would cut it with old horse clippers, right over except for the fringe – that was the style. I was bald headed all bar that fringe on the front, which stuck out under me cap. I wore a pair of the old man's trousers, cut down, with braces to hold them up. When the old man finished with a pair of trousers he would give them to one of us boys. If it was my turn he would put them on the table and tell me to lay on them. 'Up you go,' he would say. Then he would chalk round me, cut round the outline and sew them up. They looked like nothing on earth – old corduroy trousers with two buttons either side of a flap. The length depended on how old and worn they was and how much the old man had to cut off them – they might be as much as knee deep. I never had

a long pair of trousers. I wore a wool jersey on top in the
winter and nothing in the summer, except a shirt when I
was at school. I looked scruffy in me hand-me-downs, but
you weren't a boy unless yer arse was hanging out of yer
trousers.

Me shoes was hobnail boots – leather boots with studs in
the bottom of them. They was good leather and cost from
three and a tanner up to seven and six from Davies' on Upper
Street. They had iron studs in the soles and made a row when
you walked – it was no good trying to be a burglar with them
on. The chimney sweep in our road was a shoe repairer when
he weren't out sweeping and he would mend yer shoes for
a few pence a time. But Dad usually mended our boots. He
would sit there all night with a mouthful of nails – bang,
bang, bang – putting soles on our shoes. Sometimes he sewed
them on with a big needle.

One morning me brother Jim showed his boot to the old
man. 'I've got a hole here, Dad.'

Me dad looked at the boot.

'You've been hanging on the back of those bleeding carts
again!'

'No Dad, no Dad.'

But me father was furious. He aimed the boot and if it had
hit Jim it would have killed him. He threw it that hard it
went through the lath and plaster of the wall and into the
next room.

Twelve o'clock was dinner time in our house. Most days I
would come home from school and take me dad's dinner out
to where he was working. The food was held between two
hot plates tied up in a handkerchief. When I turned round
to go home he would always have some wood ready for me.
'Here you are,' he would say, 'take it on for the fire.' Coal
was tenpence a hundredweight. So the old man would

always say, 'Don't forget yer lump of wood if you want to sit round the fire.' We always brought a lump of wood home, every one of us.

Me mum cooked on an old black range that had rings, an oven and a tap for hot water. Our dinner was mostly bread and dripping or bread and jam. Me mum would get a pennorth of fat from the butcher's in a newspaper, take it home, put it on the hob and melt it down to make dripping. She knew how to make a penny do the work of a shilling and we always had something to eat in our house – but there weren't too much of it. The only time she bought fruit was at Christmas. Then we each got a tangerine, an orange, an apple and sometimes a few nuts. The rest of the year all the fruit we got was what we went and nicked, mostly from the barrows in Junction Road.

There was barrows right the way along from Archway to Tufnell Park. We could walk by the stalls in Holloway Road and all we had to do was grab an apple here, next door an orange, next a bunch of bananas. When we was very young, me and Jim would follow courting couples to Hampstead Heath and when they threw an apple core down in the gutter – bang – we would dive after it, get hold of it and eat it. That was before we knew how to pinch what we wanted.

After school we was always out till it got dark, but during the winter evenings we stopped in the warm and sat round the kitchen range. Me sisters might be sewing and me dad might be reading a newspaper or *Old Mother Shipton's Almanac*. If he ever read anything out loud me mum would say, 'That's a load of tommy rot.'

When the fire was nice and hot me mum would stick the poker in, get it red hot and put it in her jug of beer to warm it up. She didn't drink a lot but she liked half a pint of stout in the evenings. Sometimes us kids bathed in a tin bath in front of the range. We normally had a bath once a week.

We liked to listen to our gramophone with the big old horn on it, and sometimes we played musical chairs using soap boxes as chairs. On Sunday evenings me dad might have three or four hands in playing cards or a game of dice, like crowns and anchors. Me mum would play the piano, funny little bits and pieces of things. She couldn't read and write like me dad but she could play the piano. She taught Alice and Bill to play too and they took it up. Lots of people had pianos – you could pick them up second hand for five shillings.

There was plenty of pictures on the walls of our living room, of the family mostly – us kids and Mum and Dad. We took them with an old Brownie, and a bloke used to come round and take the pictures away and make them bigger. Up above the mantel was a big vase with a foot on the bottom and other ornaments that Mum kept. They was behind two velvet curtains that hung down off of brass rails. Sometimes she pulled the curtains back to show them off. Underneath was a big aspidistra plant and me mum kept the leaves shiny by wiping them with milk.

At night time, before we went to kip, we had a cup of broth to drink out of a tin enamel cup. Me mum kept a big saucepan on the go, full up with old bones and Gawd knows what else. She was always slinging in three pennorth of 'pieces' from the butcher – all the rough ends of the meat and bones. That big pot was always on the range.

Mum and Dad slept in the room off the kitchen on an old brass bed with a feather mattress. I shared a bed upstairs with Bob, Bill and Jim, and me sisters had the room next door. In the winter we would lay there under a grey army blanket with a hot brick wrapped in a scarf for our water bottle. Our pillow was a flour bag stuffed with straw. I would jiggle meself into a nice warm spot and try and get the biggest overcoat on top of me. Those old overcoats was on our backs during the day to keep us warm and on our bed at night.

VII

Winter was winter and summer was summer in them days. You knew when the snow was going to come, you knew when the winds was coming. In the winter we had snow and ice and it was very cold. In March we looked forward to terrific winds all the month. In the spring the sun come out, with all the lovely little flowers, and it got warmer and warmer. When the summer come you couldn't walk on the pavements without shoes on it was that warm.

Where I lived it was like being in the countryside. Once you left Highgate Road there was Parliament Hill Fields, Hampstead Heath and The Spaniards. Just up the road was Waterlow Park and Highgate Wood. Waterlow was a beautiful park. There was a lot of keepers there – not just one or two, dozens of them, always planting out. On the Highgate Hill side, as you walked in the gate, there was a beautiful aviary with lots of lovely birds – blimey, it was a picture to look at. The times I tried to nick birds out of that aviary, but there was always someone about.

All year, but specially in the summer holidays, I spent more time over Parliament Hill Fields and Hampstead Heath than anywhere else. As long as I come home for me food of a night time I could go out where I wanted. Kids of all ages went out all day long in the summer time. Me mum never

seen me till it was time to go to bed at about ten o'clock.
When it went dark we went to bed.

There was two estates near us where we could roam about.
Lady Burdett-Coutts had a big place hedged with trees where
we would often set our bird nets. She sold some of her land
for building Hollylodge Estate, where me father worked on
and off for years. It was a private estate with very expensive
houses and a bowler-hatted gatekeeper who always knew
everyone and who was in or out. That was where me sister
Alice went into service.

The other big place was Kenwood House, which had a
fence right the way round it – it must have had two or three
miles of fencing. I would like as many pennies as I was in
there. We would creep in to fish in the pond with cotton
reels and worms stuck on pins till we was spied by one of
the gamekeepers. The wood had lots of lovely birds in it –
songbirds, pheasants, you name it.

When I was still at school they opened the house and estate
to the public. Our school went to the opening and sang for
the King who come to plant an oak tree. There was a big
crowd there. It was a hot day and after the singing I ran
home, bought some lemonade crystals, mixed them up with
water, went back to Kenwood and sold lemonade for a penny
a cup. After Kenwood was opened we often went inside the
house to look at the rooms and the big pictures. It was free
to get in.

Me dad was never sober when we was kids, but he was a
proper father. He showed us where to go scrumping, where
to go bird catching, where to go fishing. We collected walnuts
in the season and pickled them. We made horseradish sauce
by digging down deep for the root, grating it and mixing it
with vinegar. We always had a pocket of beech nuts or cob
nuts in the autumn. We made elderflower wine in spring

and we made beez wine all year round. Dad bought the beez from the chemist shop at the bottom of our road. It looked like popcorn. We would put thruppence worth of these grains in water with sugar and watch them slowly sink to the bottom. After three months we would fish them out and it was ready to drink.

Me father had a ferret and he taught us how to catch rabbits in snares and we sold them for a bob each. We would go round with six on a stick hollering, 'Bob each, wild rabbits, bob each, wild rabbits!' Sometimes we caught birds to eat. Me dad would hang them up over the fire and eat them bones, beaks 'n'all. I caught a partridge once over Kenwood and brought it home, but me dad grumbled at me and wanted to know why I'd killed such a pretty bird. We sometimes had a duck on Sunday for our dinner. We would catch ducks on a fishing line with a bit of crusty bread – bang! – the duck would take it up and we would winch him in. He would make a good dinner.

As soon as the summer holidays started, the first thing the old man did was take all our shoes away and lock them up. We had six or seven weeks' holiday and all that time we never wore a pair of shoes or a pair of socks. We just run round barefoot.

Every day I would feed the chickens and the dogs and perhaps take the dogs round the block. Most mornings I would do some jobs for me mother too, like chop logs for the fire and for heating the water for washing. Sometimes I whitewashed the doorstep with the harstone brick which I dipped in water and rubbed on the step. It came up a lovely white. In Tiger Bay we had a little bit of pride, though we was poor. Everybody did their steps. Then I would find Ruddy, Joey Booth or another good mate of mine, George Tilley, who we called Cocker. Cocker was like a greyhound, taller than the rest of us and scrawny. The four of us was best mates.

Boys never went round with gels – it was always boys on their own and gels on their own. I didn't know anything about gels, except how to pull the bow out of their hair. Boys was boys and gels was gels. I don't think I ever knew what me sister and her friends got up to. I weren't interested. We spent all our time walking or fishing. We walked anywhere, for miles every day. We might go to Hampstead Heath, through Kenwood, then walk to The Spaniards and past the Spaniards Inn. That pub had something to do with Dick Turpin. Opposite there was a dungeon where Turpin was supposed to have lived. We went down there one day but it was just an old cave.

At dinner time we would steal some vegetables from the allotments. Once Ruddy and I was out near Manor Park Road, East Finchley. It was all country out there, with loads of allotments and greenhouses. We was hungry so we went through the allotments picking a carrot here, a brussel sprout there, and we fed ourselves with little bits of vegetables. Then I spotted a big greenhouse with tomatoes growing in it.

I says to Ruddy, 'There's some nice tomatoes there. We'll have a few of them.'

'Righto, Cabby,' he says.

They never locked the greenhouses so we just opened the door and went in. When we was inside I seen something fluttering out of the corner of me eye. It was a little wren trying to get out. Then I seen a double-barrelled gun lying on the bench. I picked it up, pulled the trigger and blew every bleeding pane of glass out the place – bang! Ruddy thought he was a dead'un, I think. The wren either flew away or got killed. Poor little bugger – they're only as big as a sixpence. I don't know what made me do it – I never even knew the gun was loaded. I just picked it up and pulled the trigger.

When we wasn't wandering round we might play football or go running on the cinder track on the heath. Or we might have a day out and walk to Hadleigh Wood, not far from Barnet, to watch the trains go by on the railway line. As they went past we would stand there in a bleeding big cloud of smoke and steam. Me mum always used to say, 'That smoke does you the world of good, breathe it in.'

We also liked to go to London Zoo. There was a canal along one side of the zoo and there was always loads of kids up on the bridge, diving into the water after pennies and ha'pennies thrown in by people passing by. They did it to see us dive and then they would stand and laugh. In we would go and scrabble round in the dirt to find those coppers. Nine times out of ten I went in nude, but sometimes I wore a pair of lady's drawers tied with a drawstring at the knee.

On one trip I was with Cocker.

He says to me, 'C'mon, Cabby, let's go in the zoo and look round.'

'Alright,' I says.

So we swam over the canal and bunked into the zoo. It was a hot day so we soon dried off. We headed straight for the monkey house. We liked watching the old monkeys racing up and down and swinging on ropes. They was lads, the monkeys – always up to something. We bought some peanuts for a penny and fed them through the bars. Then we went up to the lion house and after that to see the elephants. We never did have a ride on an elephant – it was too dear.

On the way back from the elephants we passed some parrots.

'Hang on, Sid,' says Cocker.

He was looking at the beautiful coloured parrots and he

gave them some peanuts. Then he reached over and grabbed one of them. The old parrot squawked but in a second Cocker had it stuffed inside his jersey. We walked straight out the gates with it. A few hours later we come across a bloke called Bridges who was a penny bookmaker.

'Do you want to buy a parrot?' says Cocker.

'What kind of parrot is it?' says Bridges.

'Here he is – show him, George,' I says.

Cocker got the parrot out and it started hollering and hooting.

'I'll give you two bob for it,' says Bridges.

'C'mon then, let's have yer money,' I says.

At six o'clock at night we was always home for tea. The two-handled pan would be on the hob full of hot broth. I might have that and a lump of bread and dripping. Sometimes me mum made bread pudding or rice pudding. She was an excellent cook and it was said that she once worked as a cook in the palace. There weren't anyone in the world that could cook a rice pudding like me mum. She often said about me, 'He would sooner have a basin of rice pudding than anything else!' An hour later we would be back on the heath till dark.

VIII

There was something to do on the heath all year round. In the winter there was ice skating and tobogganing. We would go on the building sites and nick some quartering and some boarding, then take it all home and make sledges out of it. We used the steel lathes from old beds for the runners. Then, when the snow come along we would drag them all up the heath and let them out at sixpence for a half hour. Every day me, Ruddy, Joey and Cocker would be up there taking the money or sledging ourselves. The run went from the top of the hill to the bottom by the bandstand.

When the ponds froze up and they give the all clear to skate, plenty of people would be over there. We hung round the ponds and nicked their skates when they wasn't looking and then we either sold them or let them out. I couldn't skate though, not even roller skate.

In the summer we would all swim. We taught ourselves to swim, just jumped in and splashed about till we could do it. There was three ponds. The first one weren't good for swimming really as it was full of leeches, but we took no notice, just brushed them off. Fishing weren't allowed there but we did it anyway, and we caught roach, carp and bream. We caught them with blood worms that we fished out of the compost in the cemetery. We caught rats too by baiting the hook with food. When we caught them we held them up and killed them with a stick. Sometimes I would take a whole clutch of ducklings from the pond and rear them at home. We would even catch swans for a bit of devilment and move them onto another pond. We took their eggs for eating, but only one from each clutch cause they was a nice looking bird.

The second pond was mainly for boating and fishing. People would take their little boats there and dogs was allowed to swim there too. Right opposite was the iron well. The water welled up red from the ground and filled up the pond. We often stopped to drink the red water. People would bring cans and bottles to fill up cause the water was good for you. They come from all over for that water.

Me father first took me to the iron well when I had sticky, sore eyes. He would bathe them and then say, 'Now drink some.' Dad was a clever old boy – he knew a lot about healing and was a popular man. There was always someone coming round saying, 'Bill, have you got this? Bill, what do you make of that?' He had a lot to do with horses in the war so people would sometimes come up and say, 'Bill, will you come up and see to the old horse, he's got the mange?' For mange he used sulphur sticks ground down to powder, mixed with a block of lard and then rubbed into the horse's coat. He always put a stick of sulphur in the dogs' water too.

The third pond was the swimming pond. It was for men and boys all week, except for Wednesdays when women could swim there. The swimmers got undressed in a fenced-off bit with partitions. We would watch them come in, see what sort of clothes they had on and follow them when they went out to jump in the water. As soon as they jumped in, back we went and rifled their clothes. If they was better than our'n we nicked them and left our old ones there for them. When I got home me mum would say, 'Where d'you get that from?' 'Off of the rag and bone man,' I would reply.

There was a concrete diving board at the swimming pond that was about thirty-three foot high. It was the first Olympic diving board. They come from all over the globe to dive from there into fifteen foot of water. One summer night we was up there fishing at two or three o'clock in the morning. We always took a big old umbrella fishing in case it rained. I picked it up.

'Watch this,' I says.

I climbed up to the top of the board and jumped off with the umbrella as a parachute. Then all me mates had to do it too.

Over by Jack Straw's Castle was more ponds – the Leg of Mutton Pond and Whitestone Pond. Whitestone was a man-made pond made out of white stone with a little wall either side. It was used as a drive through for horse and carts – anything that was pulled by a horse. The horses would go through during hot weather. As they got in deeper the water covered the hubs of the wheels. It got into all the cracks and the wood swelled. That stopped the dried-out old wheels from sounding so creaky.

I sometimes took Babs over Parliament Hill Fields first thing in the morning on me own. I always let the dog have a swim when we was over there. One morning, as we got near to the first pond, I seen what I thought was a football about twenty or thirty foot out from the edge. I threw a piece of wood in so Babs would go in and get the ball. As she got near, she went to try and grab it, like a dog would do. Then I seen it was a bowler hat. The hat went down and come up again and I seen a face. It was a man, drownded hisself. I thought to meself, 'Blimey, the poor sod's dead.' He must have been in there some time cause you don't float till after so many hours or days.

I went and found a keeper and told him there was a dead bloke in the pond. He come down and had a look then went to the swimming pond run by the head keeper. They got a punt, carried it up to where the man was, put it in the water, punted out and dragged the body in. After a while the other keepers come round and they covered the body over with a black tarpaulin. Then the police arrived with a basket trolley – a basket about six foot long on wheels that was used as a stretcher. They put the bloke on it and took him away.

Me and Babs watched the whole show but they never asked me a thing, not even me name and address. I never knew what had happened to the man. All I ever knew about him was that he would have had a good job, like in a bank. You knew what people did by the hats they wore. A butcher, a salesman or a grocer wore a straw hat. A builder wore a

soft cap. Anybody of any breeding wore a trilby hat. But
blokes with jobs in offices and banks, like the one in the
pond, wore a bowler hat with a pinstripe suit and they always
carried an umbrella.

I seen several others pulled out of the swimming pond
dead. As well as the diving board, the swimming pond had
two rafts in the middle what you could get up on and dive into
the water. Some people went to go over there thinking they
could swim when they couldn't. The keepers had a long pole
with three hooks on the bottom and they used this to fish out
anyone who went under. Several times I seen the keeper go
out in the punt and haul a dead person out of the drink.

Women could only swim on a Wednesday till a pond inside
the grounds of Kenwood was opened for women only. We
would go there and watch the gels swimming. We couldn't
get too near to them but had to stay about fifteen or twenty
yards away. They soon had a diving board there too, made
of scaffle boards and poles. A bloke called Captain Webb
arranged for it to be built for them. Captain Webb lived in a
great house up West Hill at the end of Lady Burdett-Coutts'
estate. He was more or less like the Prince of Wales as he was
very important and well known for being charitable.

The other thing we liked doing was a bit of horse riding.
The people who owned Kenwood let the Express Dairies
put their horses in the field to graze and have a rest, like.
Sometimes they was out there for a week or – if it was a poor
old horse – a month. They was pretty tame and we would
climb over the fence with an old scaffle cord, creep up to the
horse, put the rope in his mouth, jump on his back and fly
round the field. The old gamekeepers would come after us
and fire a gun to frighten us off. We would ride up to the
fence as far as we could and leap over – once we was over
the other side we was home and dry.

IX

Every summer there was an outing for all the women. They went from the Bay to Southend. That was their day out. Practically all the mums, aunts and grandmothers went. They went on a double-decker charabanc with four horses and a driver. The coach was belt driven. It had no springs and solid rubber wheels with iron studs banged in, so they was iron tyres more or less. The poor old horses dragged this forty miles to the seaside and back the same day. They stopped off at about four pubs on the way.

All the kids crowded round the coach before it went away, waving and singing, and the old gels would throw a handful of ha'pennies or pennies out. We all scrambled for these before they left. While we waved, the horses clopped away up the street on the cobblestones. Then up by Raydon Street the noise was muffled when their hooves hit the straw. There was a bloke up there, name of Bill Duggin, who had an illness what meant he mustn't hear any row. So there was a load of straw in the road round and about his house, from Buckingham's shop right down to the cemetery. What he had I do not know, but straw was often put on the road when people was ill. If someone in the street had scarlet fever or some very bad illness they would cover the street from end to end with straw so that when the horses come down they wouldn't bother them.

When the women had gone we would spend our money on sweets or ice cream. In the summer there was an ice cream pitch right outside our house. The bloke had a barrow and a churn and the ice cream was a penny, while a cup of ice and half a lemon was a ha'penny. There was a bloke selling toffee apples too. If you was lucky you got the one with the thruppenny bit stuck inside.

Sometimes we spent our money on going to the pictures. It cost thruppence and there was two sittings of a night time and a matinee in the afternoon. In the evening they had two pictures – they showed you one, then a five-minute rest, then the other one. A pianist played the piano behind the curtain. I couldn't read the captions so I just used me imagination. Before the film come on we would have a competition for the best call-out and everyone would start up. I liked to shout, 'Bob each, wild rabbits,' as loud as I could.

Not long after the women's outing us kids would go away. We went hop picking in Kent for a month every summer. We really looked forward to it. First time I went there I thought I was in no man's land. We slept in a pigsty full of straw and picked hops from dawn to dusk. We didn't really work hard, but every day we filled huge sacks with hops. We worked with some travellers who went from farm to farm picking what was in season. I went with me brothers, Ruddy, Cocker, Joey and a lorry load of other boys. A few gels come too, but not many – most wasn't allowed.

The hop picking trip was organised by Old Mother Ring. She was the moneylender for the poor in the Bay. The most you could borrow was a half crown and you paid back a penny in the shilling each week. You had to be at least sixteen to borrow money. Her old man was in the building game and she had a son called Mickey who we called 'snotty nose' – dirty sod he was. She paid us three and a tanner a week and cooked for us. We kept some of our wages and gave some to our mothers when we got back.

After work we bathed and swam in the river, and in the evenings Mother Ring made a big pot of broth with bones and rabbit so we had plenty to eat. We carried on scrumping and thieving and Gawd knows what else when we got the chance. It weren't long before we got lousy there and as soon as we got home out come the horse clippers and the red carbolic soap and off come our hair.

We was back in time for Barnet Fair when the gypsies arrived in London. It went on for seven days and seven nights. We was up there most of the time. I worked on the kiddies' roundabout, turning the wheel – I think it was a penny to go round. I would watch the old gel who owned it and when she weren't looking, nick a handful of coppers. Sometimes we took some poles and canvas up there and dug a hole for a toilet. Then we would stand by the screen and as people passed by we would cry out, 'Penny-a-piddle-or-a-poop!'

Barnet Fair was one of the best fairs in the world. It had everything – you name it, it was there. There was a horse fair and dog shows. They sold sausages and fish and chips, hot pies, jellied eels and eels and mash. There was Siamese twins in a tent and a five-legged cow – I seen it with me own two eyes. There was rides like roundabouts, swings and all that sort of thing. I didn't like the rides meself – always seemed to make me sick and give me a headache. I suffered terrible from headaches, just like me mum. There was fortune tellers sat in a tiny tent, and if you paid yer money they would tell you a load of old cobblers.

There was plenty of bartering and selling at the fair, too. The biggest money spinner was horses. Everybody brought horses – sometimes there was two or three hundred of them for sale. I would get paid a tanner to get the horse and run him up the field, perhaps a half mile, then fetch him back. Then somebody might say, 'Right, I'll have him.' It was a dangerous job cause a lot of them was wild bleeding horses.

When the fair was over everybody was running live with fleas, lice and bugs. We had to shave our hair off again to keep them down.

Even after the fair there was plenty of gypsies and tinkers knocking round London, but not all of them was the real thing. Me uncle, Tinker Day from Campbell Bunk, was a tinker. He sat on the kerb with his tinker's barrow and did his work. It had a wheel in the middle that was turned by two treadles going up and down and he used that to sharpen knives. There was a brass shade that come right over the wheel and it was always polished and clean.

Me old uncle went all over the country. If you had a hole in the kettle he would mend the hole, if the cane chair was broken he could mend that. If you had anything that wanted soldering he could do it. A proper tinker, like me uncle, could put together a broken plate by drilling it and inserting a piece of copper wire. He would tap the little rivets into the china with his hammer. He was a skilled person – you name it, he could do it.

X

I always thought, even when I was young, that I was going to make something of me life. I was very, very steady with money. If I had money I would look after it. I always kept it in a five-shilling paper bag. I liked to know I had money somewhere or other. We each got a penny from Dad on a Friday night. For that we had to do jobs like clean and polish all the knives and forks and black-lead the range. Me mum was very fussy. We cleaned the knives and forks in a machine that had brushes inside, and polished the rails of the range till they shone. On top of me penny pocket money I usually earned about ninepence a week, and sometimes more.

I was always very ambitious. If I thought I could go out and earn something I would do it, even if it meant following a horse and cart to pick up dung. I started doing that from about six years of age and I sold the dung at a penny or more a bucket, depending on how much straw was in it.

When I went round selling horse shit with me mates we also took black paint and brushes. We would say, 'Can we paint yer knocker?' If the old gel agreed, one of us would paint it for a few pence. We also got tuppence a time for polishing up doorsteps with harstone.

Me mum taught me how to make toffee apples. I cooked up the toffee, putting some vinegar in the mixture to make it nice and sticky. Then I took the toffee apples on a tray to the picture house where people was all lined up outside. I would walk up and down with me tray and say, 'Toffee apples, a penny each.' I always told them that at least five of the apples had a thruppenny bit inside – but it was only ever one.

I sold newspapers at the station, too. I helped a bloke called Peg Leg who was always selling them outside. The fight results was stamped on each paper and I had to be careful to get the customer's penny before letting him see the result.

Even on school days we was up early in the morning doing jobs, like pushing the barrows from the stables at the top of Dartmouth Park Hill down to the market in Junction Road. When they packed up their stalls at nine in the evening, or midnight at weekends, we was there to push them back up again. As well as all the barrows, there was about forty or so horses kept up at those stables. For pushing barrows we usually got thruppence and whatever we could pinch off the barrow. Sometimes they paid us as much as sixpence – it all depended how much stuff they had piled up.

If I was pushing a fish barrow up the hill I would put a big live eel or some fresh herrings down me jersey. I usually went in for live eels cause me mum used to love them. The eel would wriggle and it was all slimy. When I got it home Mum would say, 'Good boy, good boy. Now go up and get me a penny cod's head.' I would go up the fish shop and get a cod's head, bloody great big thing. Most times, if I said the cod's head was for the cat, they would give it to me for nothing. When I brought it home me mum washed it, put it in a saucepan, threw in a load of parsley and boiled it up for about two hours. Then she cut the heads off the eels, washed them clean, chopped them up and threw them in. When the liquid got cold it turned to jelly. The old gel made lovely jellied eels.

We also collected water for the flower sellers outside the station entrance. There was about a dozen altogether. They was all old women with big flower baskets, all done up lovely. We would go and get water for them or take their basket over and get thruppence.

There was plenty of blokes who come round the streets selling things from barrows and sometimes I helped them. There was the fish barrow – fresh herrings, a penny each. There was the milk barrow selling milk at a penny a pint. The milkman ladled it out of the churn into yer jug using a brass tin with a handle. In the summer the ice man come round the houses with his cart selling butcher's ice for eighteen pence a block. It was wrapped in dozens of sacks to keep it cool. I helped him for a shilling a day plus some bread and cheese.

Me brother Bill helped me get a good job one summer. He was very friendly with the woman who owned the pavilion near the tennis courts at Hampstead Heath. I was up there with him one day when I had an idea.

I says to Bill, 'Will you ask the old gel if I can sell sweets from a tray?'

'Alright Sid, I'll ask her,' he says.

She agreed and I got a deever a day to go round with a tray of sweets and chocolates. I would go all round the park shouting, 'Chocolates! Sweets!' But at the death I thought to meself, 'What am I doing this for?' I went home, hid the tray in the chicken house and never returned. Me and Jim ate all the chocolates and sweets. Didn't my Bill give me a right-hander for that!

You had to keep an ear out to earn money. Black diamonds was always in demand for burning on fires. These wooden blocks made up the roads and the trams used to run on them. When the blocks started to move or wear they took sections up at a time and we would go down and collect them. Sometimes they took the blocks up to replace them with cobbles. If I heard black diamonds was being taken up in a particular road I would go there with me barrow – a soapbox with wheels and handles. I would fill it with a load of blocks and sell them round the streets. I would sing, 'Mother dear, the log man's here, can't you hear him calling. Mother dear, the log man's here, can't you hear him calling!' Tar logs was the cheapest form of heating. There was lots of fogs in November cause everyone was burning coal and black diamonds, smoking everything out.

Me eldest brother, Bill, and Didley Tilley, Cocker's brother, had a donkey and cart for carrying firewood to sell. I was with them on a winter day when they come out of the stables at the end of the Bay and led their donkey up the incline to

Dartmouth Park Hill. It had been snowing and it was very
icy. The old donkey slipped and slid and then went right over
and bit off its tongue. We got him back inside, propped him
up on four lumps of wood and he bled to death. We danced
round that donkey singing, 'Poor old donkey's dead – poor
old donkey's dead.'

'We'll have to send for the knacker,' says Didley, when it
was stone dead.

Barber's knacker's yard come and got him and took him
away. That left Bill and Didley without a donkey for their
cart. You could buy a donkey for five shillings, but they went
out and nicked a replacement from the Express Dairies.

I spent the money I earned on food mainly. I might buy
a lump of pease pudding or a bag of cracklings from the
bottom of the fish and chip fryer. Or I would buy American
soda water, sweets and chocolate. I had a ninepenny bar
of Cadbury's fruit and nut chocolate every week, if I could,
and crept over the heath and ate it on me own. I never
shared me chocolate, but sometimes I would buy a ha'penny
bag of cough sweets for me mum from the sweet stall at
the Archway. The bloke there made them on the street. He
boiled them up and put them out on a tray to sell from his
barrow.

Sometimes I spent me money on birds or mice and little
cages for them. Or I bought baby chicks for a penny each or
rabbits to bring up. I bought a few toys too – lead soldiers for
a penny each, little fire engines and horses and carts. I had a
little jew's harp I could get a tune out of and a collection of
silk-backed cigarette cards what had pictures of film stars on
them. Me favourite toy was the magic lantern. You put a
candle inside and shone the pictures up on the wall. There
was a picture of Charlie Chaplin in there, though it was a job
to see it.

XI

When the bell went in the morning at our school, that was it – a lock was on the door and you couldn't get in and you couldn't get out. So unless you went right round the alley-way into the headmaster's office, there was no way to get into school. I often got the cane for being late. Mr Raleigh, the headmaster, would take me trousers down and say, 'Lean over there, Day.' Bang – three whips of the cane. Right little bastard Raleigh was. The only conversation I ever had with him was when he took me in the office, took me trousers down and whacked me arse with a cane. If it weren't cause I was late, it was cause somebody had reported me for scrumping, or for cheek, or for not turning up for school at all.

Raleigh was about as big as six pennorth of coppers, but a very smart man. Every morning we had a parade and he would walk up and down to see if we was clean enough. He was a right little sergeant major.

We was on parade one day when he says, 'Day! I see you wink yer eye – in the office!'

In the office I went and got the cane for it. The cane used to be split not solid and didn't it used to tingle yer, Gawd almighty. I weren't winking at all, he just didn't like me. Oh, old Raleigh was a bugger – mind you, he was a damn good headmaster, very strict.

I first went to the school at five years old and I stayed till I was fourteen. All me mates from the Bay went there. From the start I thought more about going out scrounging, picking this up, picking that up, pinching a handful of sweets or a handful of peanuts from the shop. So I played the hop more than I was at school. At the end of our school grounds there was some allotments, and me dad had one of these. Beyond the allotments there was six tennis courts. Sometimes when the people was playing we would run after the balls for tuppence or thruppence. We spent a lot of time doing that, earning a few coppers when we should have been at school. The school board officer was always round our house asking why I weren't at school.

Me school was called St Anne's. Inside the classroom our desks had an iron frame and a seat with a back to it to hold two people. The desks opened up and had two inkwells. The pen was a stick with a nib that we kept dipping in the ink. We wrote in exercise books and the teacher had a blackboard and easel. We always had to stay silent, no talking. You could hear a pin drop in our classroom.

When we arrived at nine o'clock the very first thing was prayers, cause it was a church school. We was always praying there. We had to march about three miles to St Anne's Church once a week and there was singing hymns and more praying and Gawd knows what else. That took the whole of the morning, so we had no lessons that morning, only church.

Each morning we had to do exercising – physical jerks and all that sort of thing – as if we needed it. Then we went in for lessons. We had dinner from twelve o'clock till quarter to two. That was when I went home for some bread and jam or bread and dripping. In the afternoons we might do wood-work or go in the iron foundry. I was alright at that, and at the leather work – I liked it. We made patterns on leather straps and ironed them in.

We did plenty of sports at school. Sometimes we went swimming in the afternoons at the swimming pool and bath house in Prince of Wales Road. The school had a football team and a cricket team and we played other schools, but I didn't play cause I didn't like football. I couldn't see any sense in kicking a ball and running after it. The gels played hockey and netball.

There was a couple of hundred kids and ten teachers, three of them women. One teacher was called Sharpe. He was about six foot three, a tremendous big chap, not fat but tall. I was a tearaway so I had the cane off him many a time. He would shout, 'Day!' Then I had to go up to the table and he would get the cane out of the drawer. He would say, 'Hold yer hand out straight.' Then – whoosh – down it would come.

Every day this Sharpe went through from the school up the alleyway by our house. Once I was in the garden when I see his trilby hat going along the top of the alleyway wall. I nipped across next door's garden, which belonged to Blacker, a rag and bone man who lived in the basement. I had to jump over the sacks of light bulbs that he kept for the platinum filament. I crept over to the alleyway wall, scrambled up, reached over and knocked Sharpey's hat clean off. Then I ran back to our garden and hid in the shed.

We had arithmetic, writing and reading at school but I never could do it. I would sit in lessons and listen to the teachers but it didn't interest me and the teachers wasn't bothered. I couldn't even write me name till I was about ten or twelve years old. Cocker couldn't read or write either. We didn't want to learn and so the teachers took no notice of us. We always had the job of washing and filling inkwells and things like that. When we had examinations I would just sit there and look at the others doing it. I couldn't even fill in the form.

The teachers had their little favourites and some of them passed exams or got scholarships to better schools. The young chap next door to me in the Bay, Blacker's son, passed a scholarship to go to a good college. The school bought him a uniform cause his parents never had enough money for it. They paid for his books 'n'all and he turned out to be a highly educated boy.

At the death they put me in the school garden all day. One of the reasons I ended up there was cause me goat followed me to school each day. She was a lovely old goat – only a little'un – that me dad bought me as a pet. I think he gave three and sixpence off of Boothy. This bleeding goat got so used to me I couldn't go anywhere without her. She followed me to school and made so much fuss when I went in that I was sent outside to shut her up. She made a bleeding row and cried like a baby, 'Mea-h, mea-h,' all the time. I would chain her up in the school garden to make sure she didn't eat the vegetables, and then help the gardener. The goat gave the teachers a good excuse to put me in the garden and forget about me. I couldn't do lessons but I was very good at working hard out there, digging and planting, so they taught me that at least.

I had that goat for years and she followed me everywhere. She was always with me over on Hampstead Heath. I fed her cabbages or anything what was going. Mum would put sheets out on the line in the garden and the bastard would eat the sheets if you let her.

The school grew all the vegetables for school meals. If you was very hard up you got school dinner. We grew something of everything. Sometimes there was other boys with me in the garden, but mostly I was on me own. The old caretaker did the gardening. He was a nice but very strict old boy. If you ran too fast in the playground he would stop you and he wouldn't allow no brawling. He always paraded the toilets to make sure you weren't in there too much either.

On the whole I liked being in the garden. There was nobody out there to worry you and I could go scrumping at John Bull's farm over the fence. He kept cows, pigs, chickens and had lots of fruit trees. That farm was a godsend. The fence weren't too high and there was a tree over the other side that grew fruits that was half apple and half pear. We called them squints and when they was ripe, cor, they was beautiful. I went over the fence one afternoon, got up the tree and shook it till all these squints fell down. I loaded them in me jersey and in me trousers and then I seen John Bull coming towards me. He looked like a bull too, bloody great big bloke he was. I dropped the squints and tried to run away but this John Bull caught me and didn't he get hold of me by the scruff of the neck.

I says, 'I was only releasing a duck, Sir.'

'What do you mean, releasing a duck?'

'Well, one of yer ducks was on his back and I come over here to put him on his feet, poor little man.'

'You was releasing a duck?'

'Yes,' I says.

He says, 'Well I'm going to release you, but don't come over here any more or I'll knock yer bleeding head off, boy.'

John Bull owned all the lot round there. He had a lovely country cottage and servants. Oh yes, he had plenty of money but he kept hisself to hisself. Matter of fact, nobody ever hardly seen him, unless it was in the field. I never see him out.

Another time, John Bull caught Joey Booth scrumping. He took him straight in to see the headmaster who give him the cane. He really whipped him. When Joey went home he told his mum, Mrs Booth. She come in and set about the headmaster. She was a bloody great woman and he was only small. She was effing and blinding and, at the finish, she give him a punch on the nose.

PART TWO

I

In 1926 I left school and there was a general strike. Everybody was on strike, everybody, and nothing was moving at all. Every day the Booths took their flat-bottomed cart to Archway and I went with them. We would stand outside the Archway Tavern and holler, 'East Finchley, thruppence-a-go.' People got up on the cart and sat all round with their legs dangling down, then off we would go. Well, the strike weren't nothing to do with us really – we had no work so we couldn't go on strike. We carted people about throughout the whole thing.

One day I was over at Chalk Farm with Jim when we seen a big crowd, probably three hundred people, outside the bus depot, hollering and shouting. We went over to see what was happening.

'What's going on?' says Jim to one of them.

'The blacklegs are driving the buses out.'

We stopped to see what would happen and before long a blackleg tried to get out with a bus. The strikers pelted it with bricks, stones and bottles. The bus had wire right the way round so the driver was in a kind of wire cage. That meant the crowd couldn't get to him, but they got more and more wild. The driver wouldn't stop, he kept edging forward, but the crowd wouldn't get out the way. At the death they tipped the bus right over. It made a hell of a row and there was a big commotion and a bit of fighting.

Nobody was allowed to work during the strike and that was it. The unions called everybody out. A general strike is serious, it's next to civil war. Me dad went on the scrounge – like we all did – and we never went short of anything in our house. Me dad agreed with the strike cause like everybody else he wanted more money. There was no rises in the building business. He was lucky if he got a rise about every ten years, and when he got it there was no more than a penny an hour extra.

The Welsh strikers come from Wales up to London. Thousands of them congregated in Hyde Park and had a big rally. We all went up there and had a look. The meetings went on for weeks and the strikers stayed in the kip houses. There was a place at Chalk Farm with about two hundred bedrooms. It was sixpence a night and people had to be out by eight o'clock in the morning. They did good business during that time.

The Welsh, the crafty bastards, brought little brass miner's lamps with them. They sold them for about sixpence or tenpence each, something like that – not very dear. We was supposed to buy one to help them out, but what did I want with a lamp like that? The miners found out that the London people was so generous that they stopped on and nicked all our bleeding work once the strike was over. They all jumped into the building game and never went back to Wales. That's how we come to get swamped with Welsh men.

Strikers come to London from all over the country cause London was where all the activity was. There was demonstrations and rallies everywhere – in the parks, on the street corners. Even people who lived round our way would get up on a box or stand on a barrow and start spouting off about all sorts of things. When one got up, before long there was three dozen people standing round them joining in. Some would agree, some wouldn't, and there was plenty of arguing and fighting.

There was blackshirts too standing on street corners spouting to anybody who would listen. I didn't really know what they was on about cause I didn't understand politics. I couldn't care less what was happening really, but dozens would listen to them and people would throw abuse at them, eff and blind at them, try and fight them and Gawd knows what else.

They set up their meetings in poor areas. They went to places where, if there was a hundred people living there, ninety of them was out of bleeding work. They would play on that – stand on the box and say it was the fault of the foreigners. I suppose they meant the Welsh, the Irish, the Italians, the Poles and the Maltese, who was over here by the droves. They also blamed the Jews, but I didn't take any notice of what they said. I always admired the Jew as a clever man and very hard working. They worked day and night in the clothing business. They was always at work and they saved their money – that was how they got on. A Jew kept hisself to hisself and was always down in the dungeon working.

I seen Mosley speaking on the streets once, and lots of others with their black shirts and crosses on. A bloke I went to school with, name of Don, joined them. One of his brothers was a cripple, another was a penny bookmaker and a third worked as a carpenter on film sets. His father was in Highgate Hospital. He went in ill and stopped in there voluntarily, playing the piano for donkey's years. He never done any work – lazy git – always made out he was ill. This mate of mine would stand right outside our house on an old soapbox, preaching.

In the end someone had to give in. If the guvnors had not given in they would soon have gone broke living on their capital. People went back to work gradually – different unions went back at different times, and that was the end of that.

II

I didn't feel anything about me education till I left school and thought to meself, 'What a bloody fool I am, not learning.' I was afraid to talk to some people in case I said the wrong words. I didn't pronounce me 'aiches' and sometimes I felt out of place. When I had to meet somebody, or go to see about a job, I couldn't even write me address down.

Fortunately, I could turn me hand to anything. Me first job was in a paper shop in Kentish Town. I worked there for about three months. It weren't very interesting. All I did was deliver papers and sweep up the shop – I never served any customers or anything like that. I just kept things tidy and put sweets and tobacco up on the shelves. I started at six o'clock in the morning and worked till eight o'clock at night.

A couple of middle-aged people ran the shop and they was kind to me. Me week's money was twelve and sixpence. I gave me mum ten shillings and had two and a tanner for meself. I saved it up till I had enough money to buy a decent bike. Me bike had iron carriers back and front and every morning I used it to deliver the papers. Nearly everyone had a bike and if they didn't they could hire one for sixpence a day. Me and me mates went for donkey's miles on those tykes.

Me next job was with the Co-op. I went on as a rounds boy. I was the mate to the bloke with the horse and cart. As we went along he would say, 'Half a pint in there, a pint in there,' and I would run in with the milk. After I had been there a few weeks, they give me a three-wheeled barrow filled up with milk. Instead of going round with the horse and cart I had to do part of his round with this barrow.

Early one morning I was halfway up Dartmouth Park Hill, pushing this barrow, when I looked at the barrow and I looked at the milk and I looked at the hill and I thought, 'Sod this bleeding lark.' So I let the barrow go down the hill. Down it went, all on its own, and I went home and left it there. That was the last of me milkman's job. They come round to see me old man.

He says to me, 'What happened to the barrow?'

'The bloody thing got away from me, Dad – down the hill.'

It was a monotonous bloody job, I thought.

After that I did bits and pieces of jobs, picking up some money here and there. In spring time I started selling daffodils on the pavement outside a greengrocer's for a penny a bunch. I stood on the corner by the shop with my basket, hollering out, 'Penny a bunch, fresh cut daffs.' If I did well I used to thieve thruppence out of the kitty and the shopkeeper knew it 'n'all. Well, he hardly paid me any wages.

I also did caddying at the golf course. It was eighteen holes for ninepence and a lump of bread and cheese. I had to clean their boots and clubs too for that. It was at the golf course that I met the Stewart brothers. They was friends of Bert Tilley, Cocker's brother. One was a plumber – a short-arsed, ugly looking, boss-eyed sod – and the other had a removals business. We called them both Jock cause they was Scottish.

They lived opposite the Wellington pub up Archway Hill. One of them ended up being the father to the pop singer Rod Stewart, and after Rod got famous he was still friendly with Bert and Cocker. Cocker played cards with him up at his big house and he gave Cocker a pair of red braces brought all the way from America.

One day I heard that a contractor with the name of Robert Deards was hiring workers. I got up about five o'clock the next morning, went to his yard in East Finchley and stood by the gate. Everybody was lined up there cause there was thousands out of work, hundreds of thousands in actual fact. If word went round that a guvnor wanted someone, the queue was miles long to get the job.

Before long the horse keeper come out and says, 'You, you and you – in the yard and I'll give you a job.' I was one of those what he pointed at and I got the job of chain horse boy. I got fifteen shillings a week for that and I considered meself highly paid.

Deards was a strict man. He opened the gates of the yard at six every morning. If you weren't there at six you lost a day's work. He had a big farm and a yard full of horses. He had the contracts to pull up old tar blocks and also to collect all the rubbish in the area. The rubbish people threw out was mainly ashes from the fire. Sometimes the dustbins contained glass and tins, but not a lot else. People sold rags, and everything you bought come in paper.

The rubbish was thrown into a two-wheel tip cart and then taken to the sewerage farm at East Finchley where there was a dump. They did open-cast burning up there and the ground was always hot under yer feet. That was mostly where I worked with me horse. I had to chain him on to any cart that was loaded down or stuck so that he could help pull it out.

The place was full of horses and carts coming and going

and lots of blokes sifting through the rubbish. Some men worked sieving the ash into grades – the finest went for tennis courts or running tracks or for making plaster. The rougher stuff went for building blocks. Other men worked bent double picking out the copper or tin or bones. The bones went off to the soap factory. Many times I seen a man pick up a sack of bones and a rat jump out and run right down his back. It was alive with rats up there – I never see it meself but it was said that sometimes they formed a battalion and moved along the road making a rippling river of rats. Every few months a net was put over the dump and gas pumped into it. Then the rats would pour out in their thousands and the ones that didn't die was killed with sticks.

All the liquid sewage that come into the farm was filtered through ash. The solid waste was left to go hard in big tanks. A lovely crop of tomatoes would come up on each tank from the tomato seeds that had gone through people and out the other end. They was lovely to eat. After a time the waste was dug out and carted off to farms.

I carried on as a chain horse boy till I had an accident with me horse, Bones. I was out helping to pull up tar blocks with old Bones over by the Queen's Head pub. He was an old horse with bones that stuck right up out of his coat. It had been raining and one of the carts got stuck and the horse was struggling to pull it out. I chained Bones onto the shafts of the cart to help him pull.

The two horses and the cart was right beside the tram lines. A tram come by just as poor old Bones made a slip and his hoof went under the wheels. I stood there and looked at his foot – it was a nasty cut. I thought to meself, 'I better go and tell old man Deards.'

I went back to the yard and when he see me Deards says, 'What's happened?'

'I've had an accident. The old horse slipped and went underneath a tram.'

'Blimey, back you go. I'll be up in a while for a look.'

He come up and looked at Bones and examined his foot.

He says, 'He's for the knacker's yard.'

Harris and Barber was sent for and they shot Bones in the head – poleaxed him and down he dropped. I turned me back cause I liked old Bones.

Deards says, 'Don't worry about it, boy. You can stop in the yard and help Jack.'

Jack was the horse keeper – he was a nice old boy but very stern. He could speak in a very sharp voice and he would eff and blind at me sometimes, but I took no notice. In the yard they had something like sixty to eighty horses to look after and lots of chickens running round loose. I stopped in the yard, fed the chickens every morning and swept up. I done very, very well there.

One day Mr Deards turns to me and says, 'Sandy.'

For some reason he always called me Sandy.

'Sandy,' he says, 'when you go home, ask yer father if me wife and I can adopt you.'

'Alright, Mr Deards,' I says.

I went home and me mum was in the kitchen.

'Mr and Mrs Deards wants to adopt me, Mum, cause they've got no children,' I says.

'You tell Mr Deards I'll come and punch him on the nose,' she says.

Then I told the old man and he blew his top.

Next day, I says to Mr Deards, 'Me dad says no.'

'Oh, that's alright, Sandy. Righto. You can still stay here and help Mrs Deards in the house if you want to.'

From then on I did a lot of housework for Mrs Deards instead of being out in the yard. She would give me dinner and I would clean the silver for them and do the washing up.

It wasn't long before Deards gave me another horse.

'You see that little black horse there?' says Mr Deards.

I says, 'Yeah, I see it.'

'That's Black Bess and I want you to look after her.'

I would get a paraffin rag and rub it all over her coat till she shone. Then I would paint her hooves with oil. I looked after her very well and rode her round the farm. Old man Deards would say, 'I want you to go to the field and see so and so.' Or, 'I want you to take the horse and do such and such.' Then I would get on the old horse's back and off I would go.

Mr Deards had a lot of land in Cambridge and I went haymaking there with him. He made straw and hay to sell and to keep for his horses. I stopped with him till I was about sixteen and then I packed it up. I thought to meself, 'This is a dead end job going nowhere.' You never told anyone you was going to pack up yer job, you just didn't go any more. That was it.

III

Ruddy and me was never at home – me family never knew what we was up to. Most nights we got indoors at about two or three o'clock in the morning, or we stayed out all night. If we didn't have no work we spent the day over Parliament Hill Fields or Hampstead Heath. We ran on the cinder track up there cause Ruddy had taken up boxing and he needed to do lots of running to keep in training. Sometimes we ran the length of Tufnell Park cause it was exactly a mile long. We also did weight lifting in a hayloft over the stables at the end of the Bay. A bloke there charged a penny to enter and showed us how to lift the weights – they was big, square weights used for weighing out coal.

Ruddy was a character and a half. When he was growing up, practically all he ever ate was bread and dripping, but he was very well built, a fine athlete and a great boxer. He was as strong as a lion and the sparring partner to Bombardier Wells, who was once a British champion and the man who struck the gong at the beginning of every film. He got three and sixpence for going ten rounds with him. I would wait outside for him and he would generally come out with two big black eyes, nose across his chops and cauliflower ear'oles, all for three and a tanner – Gawd almighty.

Sometimes he would try his luck at the boxing booths at the fair. When you passed by a bloke would holler out, 'Fifteen bob if you can go three rounds.' 'I'll have a go,' Ruddy would say. They would take him off and he would come back in shorts ready to fight. He'd come out black and blue with a nose like a beetroot.

Ruddy was mad on football. He went to football every Saturday. I only went to one match in me whole life, to see Arsenal.

Ruddy says to me one day, 'C'mon, let's go down Highbury, see Arsenal.'

I says, 'I don't really want to go.'

'C'mon,' he says. 'Let's go down there, kill half a day off.'

'Oh, alright.'

We goes down and watched the game standing up cause there was no seats. As I was standing watching the match, I thought to meself, 'What a game this is.' All of a sudden I got hit on the head with a quart bottle of bleeding beer.

I says to Ruddy, 'This is the first time I've come to the football and it'll be the bleeding last!'

I spent lots of time with Ruddy and me other mates at Gayler's, a coffee shop at the Archway owned by some Italians called Lucassy. Me and me mates was always in there. We would roll in and holler, 'A sav and two!' That was a saveloy, an egg and a slice of bread. You could get that with a cup of tea for thruppence. If we was hard up we would say, 'Two a-drip, all crust.' That was two slices of crust off the bread and dripping for tuppence. The crust was the thickest slice. Lucassy would say, 'How much crust do you think there is on a loaf of bread?' Tea was a penny on its own.

Gayler's was burglars' paradise. Every night they would put an awning out the front and the old man would chase us out of the shop with a broom saying, 'Go on, get outside.' He did that in case we broke the place up, cause the drinking and card playing could go on all night.

Lucassy had two daughters. The eldest was very quiet and didn't have anything to do with us. The younger one had a lot to say, though. She took a fancy to Joey Booth who was a bit of a flash bloke. He was a proper little dapper, very smart. He had a gold tooth, which was the fashion and showed you had some money. When we went in he would always say to her, 'Two eggs, rasher of bacon, two slices of bread and butter, double dose.' He loved his fat. They all fed well, the Booths. The father was the smallest one out the lot.

Joey took Lucassy's daughter up to the fields a few times, but luckily her dad never found out or Joey would have been cut into little pieces. Plenty of couples went to the heath for a bunk up. The long grass was pressed flat in places. When we was kids we would get over the fence into Kenwood at night and creep along it to listen to the courting couples in Parliament Hill Fields. If they was near the fence we would slide our arms under and try to reach their bags or coats.

On Saturdays we went to get a bath at the bath house in

Kentish Town, off of Fortis Road. It was thruppence with a towel, tuppence without a towel. There was a big swimming pool and upstairs, right the way round the pool, was little cubicles with big, deep baths. The water was lovely and hot. If you was in there too long the bloke would bang on the door and say, 'C'mon out of there, you've been in there long enough.'

Sometimes of a Saturday afternoon we would go and sit in the back garden and play cards. There might be Ruddy, Cocker and me, and Jim and his mates Meady and Snore Adams. Me dad would come in from the pub and say, 'Cut me in, lads – let's have a spill.' He would normally lose sixpence or eight pence and then he would say, 'You bastards, you've robbed me of me lot,' as if it was three quid! He was a boy, me dad.

Usually about nine or ten on most nights one of us would say, 'Shall we go down Marble Arch?' We would walk the seven and a half miles from the Archway to Hyde Park Corner. We took our time, leisurely like, and did window shopping on the way down. We went for a lark, to be in a crowd and listen to the spouters. They would be up on their old soapboxes, a group here, a group there. We went from one group to the other and took the mickey out of them and tore out a few raspberries. I was no good at arguing but me mates was very good at it. They could argue knowing perfectly well a spouter was right, but always saying he was wrong.

There was one bloke in particular I remember, a black bloke with no fingers who talked about the blacks and whites, how we used them as slaves. He lost his fingers cutting sugar canes, or so he said. He had a proper stand with a shelf on the front. He would bang on that shelf and say, 'You English bastards. We'll do to you what you've done to us, make you work for a handful of rice a day. We'll take over Britain one day.' We didn't really understand what he was talking about. We never really knew about slave trading and what they did to them.

They was all characters at Speaker's Corner. There was hundreds and hundreds of people there, not just half a dozen, hundreds, and plenty of rozzers too. When we heard somebody hollering and shouting we would think, 'Oh, something good is happening there,' and shoot across to get in amongst the crowd. Spouters started up at ten o'clock in the morning and went on all night sometimes. Some of them was very highly educated people. A lot of it was religion, the rest was all spouting about what was wrong with the country. There was women in the crowd but it was mostly men, all heckling and having a go.

Sometimes we stayed for hours at Hyde Park. Once when we was leaving in the early hours of the morning we seen the Prince of Wales, drunk as a pudding, crawling home towards the palace through the park. He was on all fours, he was that drunk. Other nights we would leave earlier and go back to the billiard hall in Archway for the rest of the night, to mark scores for thruppence a game. Or, if we was lucky and had a few bob, we would go from Marble Arch to the Lyons Corner House on the corner of Oxford Street and Tottenham Court Road for a feed. Not many hounds went in there, but me and Ruddy fitted in cause we was always well dressed. We always wore smart clothes.

IV

The fifty bob tailors' shops made beautiful suits, made to measure. The tailor would show you a load of patterns and colours and when one took yer fancy you would stop him and say, 'I like that one.' Then he would get the tape out and measure you up. 'Come back next week and have another fitting,' he would say. There was no deposit and after two or three fittings the suit was ready – all for fifty shillings. The popular colour was what they called a plum colour. If you was in full fashion the bottom of yer trousers was twenty-four inches circumference and you wore winkle picker shoes. The shoes was so pointed that when you got them on, yer toes was all screwed up inside.

Ruddy and me was looking in a shop window one day when we seen these white and brown shoes in leather. Cor, they was nice and smart. They was half winkle pickers, squared off at the ends instead of going to a full point.

I says, 'Oh Bill, when we get a few bob we'll have a pair of them, shall we?'

He says, 'Yeah, too bleeding true.'

'I'll go in and see how much he wants for them,' I says.

Inside the shop I says to the shopkeeper, 'How much is those shoes with the brown and white stripes?'

'Fifteen shillings, made to measure.'

'We might be in the weekend for a pair.'

We got hold of a few bob and went back there and each had a pair of those shoes made. Didn't we look the ticket.

Both of us dressed the same, more or less. We always had a white shirt with a detachable collar. The longer the lapels, the more you was in fashion. They was 'Vandos' or 'Vandike', or some bleeding name, and the best shirt you could buy. Hats never suited me really but we went to Dunn's, the hatmakers, and bought one each. It was three bob each for Anthony Eden hats.

We spent some of our money on clothes, but generally if we needed new clothes we would break in somewhere and rig ourselves out.

One night I says to Ruddy, 'Shall we do a tailor's tonight?'

'Yeah, alright, yeah,' he says.

'Righto.'

The tailor's had a flat roof and Ruddy climbed up onto it. There was a glass fanlight on the top and he got through and dropped down to the floor. It was, I suppose, about a twelve- or fourteen-foot drop. He got the suits and shirts and piled them all up. I looked through the window at him, then I clambered up on top of the roof and looked down at him.

'How the bleeding hell you going to get out, Bill?' I says.

'Oh, that's a point innit,' he says.

I says, 'Throw some trousers up here, throw three or four pairs up.'

I tied the trousers together and made a bloody rope so he could climb up.

We each had a suit and a shirt out of that shop and took the rest round to a family we knew who lived in the Bay, named the Cramptons. The Cramptons was proper boozers, in the pub morning, noon and night, both the old man and the old gel. The old man was a labourer in the building. His wife was a very, very big woman. She was a bugger and could she fight 'n'all. She would fight anybody in the pub – men she would fight, women she would fight, anybody. She could have took the whole street on, I should imagine.

We went down the steps to the basement of their house

and walked straight in. Everybody walked in and out of there
as they thought fit, treated it like their own home. The bedroom and sitting room was all in one behind the basement
front door, and as we opened the door we seen Old Mother
Crampton in the bed. She was always in bleeding bed, either
asleep or drunk or both. When the old man got up and went
out to work in the morning, the lodger, who was on night
work, would come in and get straight in kip with the old gel.
The old boy didn't mind the lodger sharing the bed with his
wife. I suppose he couldn't care less what happened as long
as they boozed him up, took him down the pub for a couple
of pints.

The Cramptons had five children. Frank was the eldest of
the three boys. Then there was George who suffered with
asthma and fits. When he had a fit they had to put a spoon
in his mouth to stop him biting his tongue. Many a time he
had a fit over the swimming ponds – it was all we could do
to hold him down. The youngest one, Patsy, was boss-eyed,
but couldn't he fight – he was always fighting. He was a good
mate of ours.

I says to Mother Crampton, 'Is Pat out in the back?'

'No, he's not in, but Frankie's out there.'

So we went through and helped ourselves to tea and got
talking to Frankie and his sister. We showed them the shirts
and stuff.

'Can we leave them here?' I says to Frankie.

'Alright, Cabby,' he says.

We left them there out the way so we could sell them on
a few days later.

When we got home me mum was in the kitchen.

She says, 'Where you been? Over the bleeding
Cramptons?'

Me mum didn't like the Cramptons. She thought they was

a bad influence. She said they was criminals, but we was all at it. When there was no work to be had it was the only way of getting what we wanted to have any kind of life. We wanted to dress nicely – I was very particular with me dress, I always liked to look smart – and we wanted money to go to the pub to have a drink and a good time.

Not long afterwards, Mrs Crampton got ill. Her head blew up as big as a balloon and she died of it. We heard they kept her head for experimentals.

V

The first time I ended up in court was for drinking. Ruddy and I got drunk down the Half Moon in Holloway. We was with three Italian brothers – the Cascaras – who we knocked round with sometimes. They sold ice creams on street corners in the summer and chestnuts and baked potatoes in the winter. When they wasn't selling these all three of them was boxers, and good boxers too. It was about nine o'clock at night when the shirts come off and the singing started. We sang one of our favourites, 'My Sweet Italian Maid':

> 'My sweet Italian maid,
> Now look at me, look at me,
> Underneath the window while you sleep,
> I will sing the melody, oh so sweet,
> If you only marry me,
> I'll take-a the trip, take-a the trip,
> Across the ocean,
> Back to sunny Italy,

> Then we'll lead what
> You call a great big life.
> Give you plenty macaroni
> When you're me wife,
> O-hhh, my sweet Italian maid.'

When the pub closed and we was chucked out, Ruddy and me got onto a double-decker tram to the Archway. As we went to get off the tram we fell arse over head, drunk, outside the tube station. When we looked up a copper name of Ernie Costen was standing there.

'You're nicked,' he says.

Oh, Ernie was a sod of a policeman and he was always after me and Ruddy. He was a very smart policeman but not very tall. I don't know how he got in the police force cause you had to be five foot eight to get in. We seen Ernie every day on duty outside the tube station at Archway. As soon as he seen us he would march tight to us, on our heels. He would say, 'Go on, get out, move on, move,' and he would catch our heels so that sometimes our shoes would come off. The rozzers always did this to get you to move on or assault them. Then they had a charge against you. All they was interested in was nicking you. As long as you was walking they wouldn't do anything, but soon as you stood still, that was it. Nobody was allowed to congregate over three people. They thought you was up to no good if there was three or four of you.

We went to court and I think we got fined three shillings for being drunk and disorderly. From then on Ruddy used to have it in for Ernie. He was a bugger with the police – they all knew him. If a policeman was walking towards him he would sometimes walk straight into him – bang – and give him a punch in the nose. The policeman would blow his whistle and if there was another one nearby they would try and nick us. Ruddy was very placid and it took a lot to upset him, but when he was upset you knew about it. He almost pushed Ernie through a shop window once.

People was always fighting with the rozzers – it was normal. Me Uncle Jim once hung one up from the gaslight in our street at the top of the alley. He tied a rope underneath his arms, hoisted him up and left him kicking his legs in the air. Lots of people did things like that for devilment, but they usually got pinched at the death when the Law caught up with them.

One morning we was over Parliament Hill Fields when who was coming along with his wife and his little gel but Ernie Costen.

I says, 'Look who's coming along here, Ruddy, it's Ernie.'

'Oh,' he says, 'I'll give him a righthander as he passes.'

Before Ruddy could do anything Ernie stopped and smiled.

'Morning Bill, morning Cabby. Here y'are boys – here's a tosheroon, go and get yerselves a meal.'

He give us half a crown cause he knew what Ruddy would have done to him in front of his wife. He would have knocked his block off for him.

On another day two rozzers started pushing us and we turned round to give them one. The one I hit we called Tiny. He was about six foot two, I reckon, and he must have weighed fifteen to eighteen stone. I got hold of his whistle to tug it away from him and it tore his uniform. I ended up in court. At the court there was two or three old codgers sitting at the bench saying to theirselves, 'What shall we do with him?' I got fined fifty bob and charged three pounds ten shillings and sixpence for repairs to the uniform.

A few weeks later I got drunk with Ruddy, and another policeman – not Tiny – picked us up and took us down the police station, drunk and disorderly. They put us in this cell. We had been in there a while when Tiny come in.

'Oh,' he says, 'it's Cabby Day, tearaway.' Bang.

And he give me a good hiding. He hit me on the bleeding nose and me nose went left and twisted round. It took months before it straightened out.

The police knew the Day family alright. Bill, me eldest brother, got into trouble and got the birch. What happened was Didley Tilley and Bill crept into the bakery just down the road, near the bus station in Lower Holloway. It was where all the buses stopped and garaged. They pinched a load of jam tarts and Didley went and smeared the jam part on the window when they got outside – he wrote 'Day' on it. Course the police knew who it was didn't they, and Bill got the birch for that. They dipped him in salt water afterwards and he was left with a jagged scar. Getting the birch put Bill off crime for a while. When he got better he joined the Army.

VI

I started work in a piano factory doing fly finishing. That involved putting the mouldings on the top door of pianos, then fitting the half top and hinges, then the trusses and the keyboard and lastly the backing. The backing was always in coloured linen and there was two handles fitted for lifting the piano up. It was a skilled job. Working with me was Wiggy's dad, Mr Lenny, from upstairs. He had two fingers what was always out straight – he couldn't bend them. It was an injury from the war.

Inside the factory they had an old stove called a tortoise. It had a long, flat chimney about eight to ten foot high. We used this for veneering. When we lit the fire this chimney got red hot. We put the plates on top of the chimney and rubbed fat on them. Then we put the veneer on that with another plate on top to weigh it down. We had to keep stoking the fire up with shavings and sawdust to keep it very hot. The factory was small and there was only about twelve of us working there.

About a fortnight or three weeks before Christmas we got an order in from abroad. Ten of these pianos had to be made, packed in cases and shipped away before Christmas. We worked three days and three nights without any rest to get it finished. The guvnor brought in bottles of beer and loaves of bread and cheese just to keep us going. I packed the job up after that cause I didn't really like working indoors and I could get more money dibbling and dabbling in other work and on the fiddle.

I thought a few times about going in the Army. Ruddy was always joining up. I don't know how many times he joined the bleeding Army. I joined the Army three times with him. We would go and join and then never turn up. The bloke who ran the recruiting office got so much money for every one he got in, so he was always ready to take our particulars. I had to lie about me age cause I was only seventeen. Then once we had signed the document he would give us each eighteen pence and a lump of bread and cheese. With that eighteen pence we could do a lot, like go and have a good dinner.

The last time I went to the recruiting office with Ruddy I give them me real name and address and not long afterwards they come down to see me old man.

They says, 'Mr Day, you got a son named Sidney Thomas?'

He says, 'Yeah.'

'Well, he's a deserter from the Army.'

Me dad says, 'You can do what you like with him, put him in the bleeding Army if you can get hold of him!'

They never did get hold of me. Once I knew they had been round I never went home for a while.

In the end Ruddy did go into the Army. He couldn't find proper work and so he thought it was the only thing that he could do. He went into the horse regiment of the Royal Artillery. When he come home, just after he joined, he had riding britches on. He was always a very smart chap but, oh, he looked the ticket. Whenever I seen him after that I would think to meself, 'Perhaps I should join up,' but I never really wanted to.

As soon as a bloke joined the Army, he done a little bit of training then they sent him for a stint in India. When Ruddy got back from India he spent most of his time in the glass house, the punishment quarters. The glass house was a terrible place to go and Bill was in there five or six times. They give him sixpence a week to buy shoe polish, cleaning gear, toothpaste and personal things, but he would spend it all on a slab of chocolate. Poor old Bill, he kept on getting more sentences. He just wouldn't do anything that he was asked to do. 'Cabby,' he would say to me, 'it's murder. I always have to be at attention. Yessir, nosir, three bags full sir, all that lark.' When he got mad enough he would do a bunk. He was always deserting and he would come home for a while till they grabbed him in the pub or billiard hall and put him back in the glass house.

One particular time when Ruddy was home on desertion from the Army we decided to go out for the day. I waited for him at the back of the tube, at the Junction Road end. There was always at least a hundred people standing round – bookmakers, flower sellers, paper sellers, vegetable sellers – you name it, they was there. All the hounds, the villains, met on the forecourt to play cards, dice and a game called 'Down the Pile'. It was a penny a go and winners was paid out two to one. The bloke had about twelve pennies in one hand. He took three off, one at a time, and you had to guess what order they would come out – like, head, head, tail – to win.

You weren't allowed to gamble, that was the law. But the bookmaker was always there just the same, waiting for the bets. As people walked past he would hold his hand behind him saying, 'Put it in me outer.' Everyone who was out of work always went round there to see what was happening. If you was skint, had no money at all, you could get thruppence for being a lookout to warn them if the rozzers showed up.

Another game was two ha'pennies on the stick. Each player put two ha'pennies on the stick – one, two – and threw them up in the air. They went up, twisted and landed down on the ground. The man what threw two heads was a winner. There was always a game of dice going on, too. The thrower squatted down in the middle and when he threw a winner he kept the bets; when he threw a loser he had to pay them out two to one. If he wanted to pack up he would say, 'I'm skint – take the dice over,' and someone else would take it over. It was a fiddling game for anybody who had a pair of loaded dice to substitute for the real ones. All the out-of-works played these games. They was gambling games for the poor man. It was part of yer life.

When Ruddy turned up we crossed over to the Archway pub. There was people everywhere, busy. The pull-in outside the pub was a resting place for horses before they had to go up the Archway Road. When they done with tar logs and put stone cobbles down, the poor old horses couldn't go up

Archway Road straight, they had to zigzag. It took them twice as long to pull the cart up then cause it was twice the journey.

Buses and lorries pulled in outside the pub, too. We caught a lorry going north, climbed up on the back without the driver seeing.

I says to Ruddy, 'Let's go to Newmarket, see what we can get up there.'

'Righto, Cabby.'

We got near enough to Newmarket when the lorry stopped, so we started to walk. We was going up a bit of an incline, a steep hill hedged with ivy. Halfway up was a milk float with all the milk bottles in it.

I says to Ruddy, 'Let's have a quart of milk each.'

We had our quart of milk, drunk it, threw the bottles in the ditch and started to walk on. I suppose we done about a mile when all of a sudden a little open-topped Austin Seven drew up alongside of us and four bleeding great burly rozzers chucked out.

They says, 'You stole milk out of the float down the road, didn't you?'

We says, 'Y-yeah.' We didn't argue.

'And you threw the bottles down in the ivy, didn't you?'

'Yeah.'

So we pleaded guilty more or less. They took us to the station and then on to some prison, I forget where it was. We got seven days' detention in there and then Ruddy had to go up to the high court where they done him for desertion as well. He got three years at Portland prison. Three years for desertion and a quart of milk. I got a caution.

Ruddy spent more time deserting than he did as a soldier. The three years at Portland got him out of the Army for good.

VII

There was times when there was hardly any work. If you was out of work you had to sign on two days a week at the Labour Exchange. Everybody had to pass a means test. They asked what you had in yer home and if you had any money in the bank or savings. If you told them, for instance, you had a piano, they would say, 'Well you don't need that, you can sell it.' Then you had to sell yer piano and anything else you had of any value before you could sign on.

The Labour Exchange was in Seven Sisters Road. I should imagine there must have been at least five hundred to eight hundred in the queue sometimes. The queue was there all day and it was eight men across. Mounted police went up and down to keep them in order. Women had a separate queue round the back. There weren't many women working really. There was no work for the men so the women didn't have a chance.

I rarely went to sign on. I was out of work for long periods but I didn't like getting handouts. I had the brains to help meself to what I needed. I was enterprising like me dad. If I ever went to the Labour Exchange I went with me mates. We stood there in the queue and had a smoke, a chinwag and a lark round. It took about two hours to get seen so there was plenty of time for talking about what we had done and what we hadn't done. Inside the building there was a great big counter with eight or ten people behind. When I got to the front I would say, 'Have you got a job for me?' Then the bloke would look down the sheet and say, 'Oh yeah, there's one here, it's so and so.' So off I would go with a green card.

If you never got the general foreman's signature on that piece of paper, whether he took you on or not, you lost yer dole.

At that time a labourer got two pounds, twelve and six-pence a week. The dole was twelve and sixpence a week and men with families could apply for Parish Relief to get food and clothes tickets. It was just about enough to feed you but not to pay the rent as well. It was hard enough to do that if you was working. That's why so many didn't pay their rent. In the Bay landlords had given up asking for it. The last time we seen our landlord he had come round to the house to talk to Dad.

He says to Dad, 'Give us twenty quid and you can have the house.'

The old man says, 'I ain't got twenty bleeding pence, no mind about twenty quid.'

So he give up coming round looking for rent.

People had to do what they could to help theirselves, specially if they couldn't work. An old cripple, Mr Coker, lived next door to us above Blacker and his family. He made wavers for the fair, hundreds of them. He also kept a celery barrow outside his house on Saturday and Sunday. His sons went to King's Cross to fetch the celery and mustard and cress and he kept it all out in the garden covered over with sacks. That was how he kept going.

There was a place you could go when times got really hard – the Salvation Army. They would give you a meal or a loaf of bread or clothes, things like that. The Salvation Army drill hall was right opposite me house. Sometimes there was a bit of a queue, but mainly you could just go in, get what you wanted and come out. It was like a big jumble sale inside.

Opposite the Archway, front entrance, there was a building for out-of-works to go and mend their boots. They gave out pieces of leather and provided nails and a hammer so people could mend their own boots and put new soles on them.

There was no other help at all, none whatsoever. Some people who was out of work and couldn't pay their way had the bailiffs round. If the landlord put the bailiffs in, their furniture was automatically thrown out onto the kerb. There was always people getting evicted, and I often seen whole families sat with their furniture on the side of the road. Usually relations or neighbours took them in and made room for them till they got somewhere else to go. I seen the bailiffs go in every day of the week practically. They had no sympathy for anybody.

There was plenty of tramps knocking round in the parks sleeping rough, and plenty of beggars. Beggars could get pinched, and if they got caught it was three months in the nick – although at least it was warm. If I had any money I would sometimes give two or three coppers to a tramp for a can o' tea. I always said 'Hello' to Long Jim, who sat outside St Anne's Church all day drinking out of his old tin can. He sat on the same bench every day and slept on it at night. He must have been about six foot seven and his feet was wrapped up in paper. They stank like merry hell. Everybody in Highgate knew Long Jim. After I had sat for a while and had a chinwag with him he would say, 'Go down and get me a pennorth of tea, boy.' Then I would go and get the quart can filled up for him.

Any tramp who wanted a night's sleep could go to the Sally Army workhouse, but if they stayed there they had to make brushes or chop wood to sell in their shop. Anyone who had no work and really had nothing or nobody – mainly old people – could get into the workhouse. Me Uncle Jim wound up there cause he never married and he had no kids to look after him. All the people in the workhouse wore a grey overcoat and a cap.

When times was bad people helped each other. If there was anything going people would tell each other about it and we would all go after it. Or if they had something they didn't want they would give it away. But it was most important to help yer family out. If I got hold of any money I would give some to me mum or the old man. I had a gold watch once what I picked up.

I says to the old man, 'You want to buy a gold watch?'

'Gold – where is it?' he says.

'I'll show you.'

'How much do you want for it?'

'Give us a tosheroon and you can have it,' I says.

He give me the half a crown, took it up the pub and sold it for fourteen quid.

When he come back he says, 'I got fourteen quid for that watch.'

'Good luck to yer!' I says.

Cocker and me had some luck ourselves one evening. We was going along Junction Road past the costermongers and their barrows. As I went past one stall I nicked a hand of bananas and the bloke seen me and chased me. I ran up Junction Road and Cocker followed on. The bloke give up after a while and we carried on towards the back of the tube station. As I stopped and caught me breath I looked down and seen a purse on the pavement. I thought to meself, 'Cor blimey,' and I picked up the purse and put it in me pocket.

When we got home to Cocker's house we had a look in it. There was three pounds ten in it. Hang me, we was rich! Poor old George's mum was in bed dying and had no gas for the lights, so we put some coins in the gas meter to keep it alive and then we split the rest between us. It was a godsend that purse. Cocker put some of his share in his usual place – under the sandpaper at the bottom of their birdcage. Not long after his dad found his hiding place and helped hisself to the money.

VIII

The Booths had a stall in North Finchley where Mother Booth sat most days. Sometimes Joey and me looked after her stall for a half hour. We would thieve two and six while we was there – that took us a long way. Then Joey's brother, Georgie, opened a café in North Finchley where he had a one-arm bandit. I knew a bit about one-arm bandits. I knew how to take the back off and put me finger up inside and push three springs to empty the machine. Me and Joey used to raid it when we was left in charge. George used to wonder what happened to the money.

The Booths was all looked after in their house by the only gel in the family, Louie Booth. She never hardly see daylight, poor little cow. They had plenty of money. Every Christmas at the Booths' shop the barrel organ come out and there was a singsong and a booze up. They lived well.

The Booths asked if I wanted to help out on their market stalls and soon I was doing it regular. Every week, on market days, Joey and me went to Rugby, Sudbury, Tring or Oxford. We made a lorry out of a big Armstrong Siddeley car – a bloody great big thing. We took the seats out and fixed a twelve-foot barrow board on top so we could load up the fruit and vegetables. We would leave Finchley at midnight to get to market. The Armstrong Siddeley couldn't go fast and had a lot of weight on so it would take hours to get there. Joey done the driving. The lorry did about walking pace and sometimes – for a lark – he got out and walked by the side of it, leaving me in the passenger seat. 'Alright, Cabby?' he would say and grin at me.

That poor old motor – didn't it have to do some work. Once we put so much weight on it that the tyres split. On the way to market we always picked ferns out of the hedgerow to use in our display. When we got there we would unload the boxes and stack up all the fruit and vegetables neatly on the barrow with the best at the front and the worst at the back. It looked a picture with all the colours of the fruit and the tangerines wrapped up individually in red and silver paper. At Easter time there was all the beautiful salad crops that were in season as well. Tomatoes was tuppence a pound, apples a penny a pound, thirteen bananas for a shilling. We spent the whole day weighing up – we was always busy cause ours was the cheapest stall.

Joey's brother Billy knew a few tricks. Some apples come in boxes with each apple wrapped in paper. Billy would buy a few bushels of small Bramleys, shine them up with a cloth, wrap them in paper and sell them as Orange Pippins. He would also go up to King's Cross to the potato market and buy two or three tons of small potatoes, then bring them home and scrub them in a bath. When they was clean we helped him pack them in boxes used for new potatoes. We put them in wet so the peat stuck to them and nailed the lids down. When we got them on the stall we would cut the wire and break open the box so people thought they was genuine new potatoes.

At Christmas we sold dried dates from the year before, bought cheap as leftovers. We spent hours lifting the lids of the boxes, pulling the paper back and painting the dates with treacle so they looked fresher. Then we would sell them as new crop dates.

All the old gels come out shopping on market day. We would sing out the wares as they went by: 'Fourpence a pound BramMMM-ley apples; eat, roast, bake, boil, make a puddin' or a pie, a tart or a turnover!' At seven or eight o'clock at night the prices would come right down on the stalls and in the shops. The butcher might stand with a toffee apple for a hammer and tap on the window as people walked by saying, 'Eighteen pence the whole lot, eighteen pence for a whole leg of lamb.' As it got later, the prices kept going down and down and all of us would practically give it away at the death.

We packed up at ten o'clock and went home. At the end of the week I got me wages of twelve shillings and a tanner and what I could fiddle. I normally fiddled another twelve and six a day so I was a rich man. Joey knew I did it. If we was having a bad day, Joey would turn round and say, 'Cabby, don't do it too strong today – the game's bad.' 'What do I want to rob yer brother for?' I would say. 'You would rob yer own bleeding mother!' he would reply.

Once on the way home we was going from Muswell Hill to Hornsey in the Armstrong Siddeley when the brakes failed. We went tearing down the road and straight through the window of the Express Dairies shop. Crash, bang, wallop, we was in the milk shop! Joey was a mad brain driving. He just backed out and we carried on home.

Another trip we seen a young bloke of about eighteen hitchhiking.

Joey says, 'You want a lift?'

'Yeah, please, mate.'

'Jump in the back then and cover yerself over with the tarpaulin.'

There was only enough room in the cab for a driver and his mate. I was the mate and Joe was the driver, so this bloke hops in the back. We was going to Oxfordshire and when we got there in the early hours he was as stiff as a poker, frozen solid, poor sod! The bloke was called Eddie. He was a rough and ready, round-faced Irishman and a hard worker. He ended up stopping with the Booths for years.

We bought the fruit and vegetables at Covent Garden and sometimes at Spitalfields. Covent Garden was the heart of London. There was a place there that had any costume for all the film sets – you name it, they had it. Anyone theatrical used to hang out in the bars round Covent Garden. Anybody who was anybody knew Covent Garden and plenty went there to buy booze all day and night. The pubs never shut and we often went in at four in the morning for a rum and coffee.

Each shop had a big cellar for storage. Everything that was from abroad was seasonal. You couldn't buy oranges at certain times of year. Bananas come in green and they would hang them up on the rafters down in the dungeons. There would be about a hundred stalks of green bananas under gas lamps and after two or three days they would come out yellow – that was how they ripened them. The Canary bananas always come in a crate, two stalks in each crate, with paper and straw round them for protection. They was the best in the world, lovely.

When Spanish grapes was in season they come in barrels sealed with cork. We would go down to the cellar, open up a barrel, stick a hand in and squeeze a few bunches to make the cork wet with juice. Then we would go upstairs and say to the sales bloke, 'How much is those wasted grapes?' 'What do you mean wasted grapes?' he would say and come down and have a look. Where they was five bob for a barrel we could get them for a shilling by doing that.

For half a crown the cart minders would go off and do buying for people. They carried out the full bushels and took them back empty. Sometimes they had bets on how many empty bushels they could carry. Some could carry as many as twenty and they would be as high as a house. The police would dish out badges to minders and they was crooked. I would hear them say, 'Righto, cough up, put it in me outer.' If a minder never bunged the policeman he never got a badge. But the minders did very, very well there so it was worth it to them.

Once me and Joey bought some very ripe bananas from the market. We took them home, mashed them up in a bucket and pressed the mixture into little wooden pots – the kind that chemists used. Then we took the pots to Caledonian Market and Ruddy and Cocker come along too. When we got there Cocker sat on an orange box and took off his shoe. He rubbed his foot till it was reddish looking and then I carefully applied some of the banana mash to his big toe.

'This way me dears for yer corn cure!' I says.

'Oh, me poor old feet,' says one old gel. 'I'll have a pot.'

Old Cocker was the best one for that game. He was a right old pan face. He wouldn't smile no matter what was said to him. He was the one to make the silly old sods believe in our corn cure.

IX

It weren't long before I thought to meself, 'Well there's not much in this lark with the Booths and I'm not earning enough money.' So I packed it all up. Me old man heard about it.

'Right,' he says, 'back into the building game.'

I first went into the building lark when I was about sixteen, just after I finished working for Old Man Deards, but I never stopped in it. I was a teaboy on me dad's site. The blokes had two cups of tea a day and paid me sixpence a week each. I had to make the tea, wash up all their cans and keep the mess room tidy. I would buy me tea, tins of milk and brown sugar on a Saturday. Every morning I would find some bits of wood, build a nice big fire and set up a tea cauldron over it.

Towards the end of me first week me tea supplies was getting low.

Me dad says, 'Here's what you do, boy – they won't know the difference.'

He threw a bit of washing soda in to turn the tea darker and then a lump of pine wood to take away the taste. I used that trick every week after that.

After being a teaboy I did a bit of barrow running. It was very, very hard work cause the barrows was bloody heavy. As the builders dug a trench to lay pipes we put all the mud in the barrows, run it away and tipped it up. Sometimes I ran barrows of concrete when they was laying floors. The cement was made of ash and lime, and for concrete we mixed it with crushed baked clay. This clay was made by chopping down a tree, setting fire to it and baking the clay earth round it. Then this was broken into little bits.

Me old dad always had a flattened out old spoon tucked in a strap on his leg like all the other navvies. He would use it for scraping the clay off the spade. Then he would dip the spade in water so it would go through the earth like butter. He was rarely out of work cause he was a clever man in the building business, although he was only classed as a labourer. He could do anything – you name it, he could do it. He was a good pipe layer, a good scaffler and he always wound up on the building site as the foreman.

Lots of me family was in the building – me brothers some-times worked with Dad, and Uncle Jim, his brother, worked with him as a hod carrier. Jim was a very quiet old boy who lived on his own in our street. Me cousins, Bob and Sid, the sons of Uncle Bob Draper who got his jaw blown off in the fourteen war, also worked with me dad sometimes. He was a hard task master. When you worked with him you knew you was there to work and that was that, no larking about. When me dad was foreman on the job nobody could get away with nothing, specially his family.

I decided to take me dad's advice, but I wanted to do something better than labouring so I spoke to me brother, Bill.

'If I get some bricks can you teach me how to lay bricks in the garden?'

'Yep,' he says. 'Bring home some bricks and I'll show you how to do it.'

Bill taught me how to lay a few bricks. We laid bricks as if we was building a house or a wall. Then I went into the building proper – that is how I come to get me trade.

Me very first job as a bricklayer was at Morden, at the end of the tube line. I would go out there on me dirty tyke. Wills the builders had a big job there – a seven-mile square plot of land for council houses. They was building a big estate with its own railway to bring in materials and a shop. Me brother Jim was working there and he spoke to the foreman for me, Mutton Eye Bill they called him. I had to give old Mutton Eye seven and sixpence a week to keep me job cause I weren't a full-blown bricklayer. A foreman had a lot of power – he never spent his own money in the pub.

Me wage was one and ninepence ha'penny an hour. As it was what they call 'field ranging' – meaning out in the sticks – we got a penny an hour more than the normal building rate. We worked hard in all weathers, except when it was too cold and frosty for the cement to set. Then we had to stand round smoking Woodbines and playing betting games till it warmed up. No matter how hard it rained we kept going – even when the rain ran in rivers down our arses.

One Saturday we was queuing up for our wages and blokes was pushing and shoving as usual cause they was eager to get down the pub. Some poor bugger got pushed and stepped onto the railway line just as a train come past. He got his leg sliced off by the train. Another time a bloke was pulling up a barrow on a wire bond. The wire was wound round a drum that was turned by a tractor. He put the chains on but the barrow jerked as it went up and he was hit on the head by a brick. Building could be a dangerous game.

Lots of firms wouldn't hire you if you didn't have a Union ticket. It was eighteen pence to get yer ticket and sixpence a week after that. The ticket steward would say, 'I want to see yer card,' and you had to show him yer card. If a bloke never had one then the steward would say, 'Off you go.' I thought it was wrong that you had to pay sixpence a week to belong to them and you had no choice. I didn't always bother with a ticket but it was handy to have one. Once I owed about twelve shillings on me ticket and I decided to go and pay up. At the Union Office there was three blokes behind a table. Just as me turn come one of them bent down to get a bottle of whisky and have a drink. A bottle of whisky was about twelve shillings.

I says to the bloke, 'You're not getting a bottle of whisky out of me. You can stick yer ticket.'

After Morden I helped build some of the finest houses in Finchley – in Bishops Avenue, an up and coming place. The houses was all very expensive, with a lot of land to them and lovely gardens. They called it millionaire's row. It was the only road where you could find a policeman twenty-four hours a day – they was never without a policeman up there. The people what lived there was top notches, nearly all of them Jews. We built houses for Billy Bunting, Steve Donahue, the champion jockey, and Gracie Fields. When we was topping out her house Gracie Fields come along to have a look at it. Her house was beautiful, all white bricks. Each house cost about five thousand pounds, which was a hell of a lot of money.

I learnt me trade with that firm. They put me in what they called the cutting shed, where we cut red rubber bricks for arch building or any design of brickwork. I stopped in there all day long cutting arches for those houses. Most of them had tuck pointing. The brickwork was filled in with black sand and cement and then a white cement was put on with a very thin trowel. The white was tucked onto the black and the house looked black and white when it was finished.

Most of the time I didn't have regular building work – I did whatever work was going. One summer when I was out of work I went to the Labour Exchange and got a job pointing the waterworks near Oxford. I was took on by an old boy who lived in Holloway. He had the job priced for so much a yard. We lived in a bus by the river for four months and punted up the river to the waterworks each day. The old farmer who rented us the bus gave us the punt to use. Twice a week he brought us down a churn of water, a half dozen eggs, a lump of bacon and milk. The bus was a proper bus, seats 'n'all. We turned the seats round downstairs and put boards on them for a table and we kipped on the seats upstairs. We cooked on a primus stove.

When we got back from work each day I spent me time swimming and I was as brown as a berry. I would get on top of the bus and dive into the drink. I swam in the nude, never had no costume or nothing. One evening I was on top of the bus, just about to dive in, when round the bend come a boat load of young ladies from Whitney Blankets Factory, out enjoying theirselves. I jumped in quick to get away from them but the water was so clear I had to get out cause they would have seen me. I scampered up the side of the bank to get back inside the bus.

The old boy says to me, 'Hide yer bleeding self before they see you.'

But it was too late. 'Oyyy oi!' they hollered out.

We worked from first light in the morning till the evening. At the weekends we walked a mile and a half to Oxford to catch the bus back to London. I don't think I ever walked round Oxford itself – I was too keen to get back to London. It cost one and sixpence return from Oxford to the Archway Tavern on a Greenline bus. First thing I did when we got in was go in the Archway Tavern for half a pint of beer. Then I would go across the road to Gayler's and have a cup of tea, sav and a slice, lovely. Then I might go to the billiard hall to find me mates.

It was at the billiard hall that I met Chazzer later that summer. His father was a union official and his family was quite well off. They had a nice house in Hornsey somewhere – but he was a villain like me.

PART THREE

I

When I was twenty years of age I says to Chazzer, 'I ain't never seen the sea.'

'Ain't you?' he says.

It was only forty miles away at Southend so we decided to go. There was a lorry that went from Highgate owned by a bloke name of Cane, Chinny Cane. He was a fighter at the thirty bob fights in the Blackfriars ring, but practically every Sunday he took people to Southend. So the next Sunday we paid sixpence each, jumped in the back of the lorry and off we went. Me, Chazzer, Ruddy, Cocker, quite a crowd of us went down there for a booze up.

Halfway between London and Southend there was a bloody great pub called the Halfway House. That was a proper place where you could go and get drunk and enjoy yerself. There was always hundreds of people there on a Sunday. We pulled into the big forecourt and stopped there for a few, then we went on to Southend. We stayed there till about half one in the morning when the lorry took us home again. As for the seaside, I didn't think anything of it. I was that bleeding drunk I lay spark out on the sand till the sea come in and woke me up.

Southend was a day out but we spent most weekends in our local pubs. The Brookfield and the Totnes was nearest to the Bay. The Brookfield sometimes stayed open late. The landlady would say to us, 'Hang on, boys, I'm having a bit of a ding dong.' Upstairs we would go for pints of beer or Guinness.

On one occasion she brought out some champagne for some celebration or other. After we left the pub we ended up drunk as lords in Highgate Cemetery. The railings had spikes on but we weren't very fat so we squeezed through. Inside was a full-size marble piano. Ruddy sat on the stool and made out like he was playing a tune and we stood round singing, dancing and yelling. The bloke who looked after the place lived nearby in the gatehouse but he never come out at night – he was too afraid to chase us off and we was only having a lark.

The Half Moon in Lower Holloway was a good night out if you wanted singing, but the best one for that was the Distillery on Upper Holloway Road. It cost a penny to get there on the tram and they had some lovely turns of a Saturday and Sunday night. They never charged anything – they just wanted to sell their beer. There was a room with chairs and tables and a stage for comedians and singers. The singers would sing all the latest songs, we would buy them pints for their pay and we would all end up as drunk as lords.

The pub we went into the most was the Cat on Highgate Hill. We was always drunk and playing darts to all hours in there. They sold any beer you liked on draught. Mann 'n' Crossman was popular cause it was the cheapest beer, sixpence a pint. We all liked a drink, except for Cocker who was not a big drinker. Chazzer was the worst – he would drink pint after pint of bitter. Bitter was the strongest drink you could buy apart from whisky.

One night in the Cat I says to him, 'Chazzer, you'll regret it one day, you'll wind up in the snake pit, drinking meths.'

'Naw,' he says, 'I just like a pint.'

'You like a pint too bleeding much,' I says.

I got very, very friendly with the guvnor's wife at the Cat. She took a fancy to me cause her husband was an alcoholic and all he ever wanted was a bottle of whisky. I would go upstairs with her and have a cup of tea. One night she tried to give me a kiss in the passageway, but that kind of thing weren't up me alley at that time. All I was interested in was getting me living or going out on the fiddle so I had money to buy nice clothes and keep meself properly.

The billiard hall in Holloway Road was another hang out. Sometimes Chazzer and me would sit in there playing rummy for three days without coming out. The place was managed by old Bootnose and he had ten tables – it was sixpence for a half hour. He was a big, tall geezer with one hell of a hooter. He had what looked like a tennis ball hanging on the end of his nose. Gawd, he was well looking. Next door to the billiard hall was the Hole In The Wall – a kind of shack where you could get tea, bacon sandwiches and rock cakes twenty-four hours every day of the year bar Christmas Day.

I seen a man called Ernie Tappin lose his shop on the billiard table once. Ernie was playing a bloke called Kirby. This Kirby was a good player and so was Ernie. They played for a long time and at the death Tappin had no money left.

Kirby says, 'I'll lay you this much money to yer shop.'

Tappin says, 'Alright, yer on.'

He had been left the shop by his old man who hadn't been dead a year, and he lost it right there on that table.

Near the billiard hall was a place called Dodger Hilliar's kip house run by an uncle of mine, Charlie Day. Lots of Irish navvies stopped there so they could work locally. It was a stinking place and it cost sixpence a night. We slept there many a night when we was too drunk to go home. We would roll in drunk as puddings and tip all the blokes who were in kip out of their beds for a bit of devilment.

At the weekend we sometimes went to the dances held in schools or in Army drill halls, like the Salvation Army hall right opposite me house. It was a lovely building in red brick what took up the room from the corner of Raydon Street, right down to the alley in Balmore Street. As kids we had played there, swinging on the iron railings that went all the way along and climbing down the steps to the airy below.

It was sixpence to get a dance at that hall and there was no beer allowed. Gels mostly drank lemonade anyway. Except for the old gels, women never drunk a lot cause they never had any bleeding money to go out drinking. Inside the hall a load of hounds would be on one side of the hall and a load of gels the other side. There was no tables and chairs, only what we called a tin band playing at one end. As we went in we looked at all the gels and went thumbs up and winked to each other. I weren't a dancer – I didn't know what foot to move first and me mates was the same. But some blokes was mad on dancing and all that game. I knew two blokes, Bill Windsor and Bill Frost, who went regular to the sixpenny hops at the Palais to go dancing.

On a night out we always dropped in to the Archway Tavern first. Everyone went in there – it was a meeting place. One night I was standing outside the pub with Chazzer when a lorry from Liverpool pulled up and a hitchhiker jumped out of the cab.

He says, 'Where's the best place to get a cup of tea round here?'

'Gayler's, mate, over there,' says Chazzer.

'Where's the nearest billiard hall?'

'It's in Holloway Road.' And we gave directions.

Off this stranger goes to get a cup of tea and we went to our dance. A few weeks later he was running a penny book in the billiard hall. That bloke turned out to be William Hill, and that is how he got started in gambling.

Gentleman Jim, the all-in wrestler, come to London the same way as William Hill – on a lorry to the Archway. He was a very slim bloke and a hairdresser by trade. He set up a barber shop near us in Raydon Street. Then a couple of years later he got interested in wrestling.

'Cabby, that's the game for me,' he says.

'Righto, Jim,' I says.

So he put weight on with pints of Guinness and oysters, trained hisself up and wound up a very rich man. He was called Gentleman Jim cause he always dressed very smart in silk dressing gowns and talked posh. He took a fancy to me sister Lulu. He was always coming round and I had to put me foot down.

I says, 'You keep away from me sister, you randy old sod. Don't come round our house any bleeding more.'

I liked him but I knew he was a wrong'un and I was right to warn him off. What did he do? He drank hisself to death.

II

The first girl I kissed was called Maxie. She had rusty, shoulder-length hair and weren't bad looking. She lived down the street as a lodger in me aunty's house and worked doing housework. She did all the running. I suppose she thought, 'He's not a bad looking geezer, I'll collar him.' She weren't a bit shy. I took her out to the pictures and to pubs but I hoofed it when she got too keen.

It was Maud next door who really took me fancy. She was a beautiful looking girl and always smartly dressed. She had lovely red hair and a nice figure. But she wouldn't have any truck with me. She married Chinny Cane who wound up punch drunk and a wino.

Chazzer's sisters was nice, good looking gels too – but I weren't really interested in having a girlfriend. I didn't have time for one. Chazzer, on the other hand, was always out after gels. They thought he was good looking cause with his moustache he looked like a proper Clark Gable. Practically every evening Chazzer was out on the 'monkey parade' on Highgate Hill. That was where all the young ladies walked looking for a husband. Chazzer was up and down a thousand times a night tailing them. 'Ooo, look, Cabby,' he would say, 'there's a decent bride.' Then he would go over and chat her up.

Then it just so happened that one day we was walking from Gayler's to the Archway when I seen two gels, round about sixteen years old, getting onto the bus to East Finchley. One of them had beautiful long blonde hair right down to her bum. She had on a straw hat cocked on the side. She looked better than any film star.

I says to Chazzer, 'C'mon, get on that bus.'

'Why?' he says.

'To follow those gels. I want the blonde one – you can have the other one.'

It was tipping down with rain, pouring, and I was wearing me good suit and me trilby hat. The brim of me hat had turned down over me ears, pouring water all over me. We jumped on the bus and sat down in front of the gels. I took off me hat and I thought to meself, 'I bet I do look bleeding well.'

I says, 'Can we walk you home?'

The blonde one says, 'We only live by the bus stop.'

'Well can we go for a walk anyway?'

We got off the bus and walked about a hundred yards down the road with them. Then I went one way with the blonde gel and Chazzer went the other.

'What's yer name?' I says.

'Mary, Mary Ball.'

We walked to the Manor pub and then turned round and walked back to the top of her road.

'Mary,' I says. 'Can I see you tomorrow?'

'Yeah, alright,' she says.

It weren't till later that I pieced two and two together and realised who she was. I already knew her family from years ago. When I was only about fourteen I had been walking past the Archway pub when I seen a bloke outside, a big fat man with ten horses tied head to tail. I could see he was a horse dealer who had just come from the Elephant and Castle horse sale.

I says to him, 'Do you want a hand with them, mate? Can I drive them home for you?'

'It's a long way, East Finchley,' he says.

'I've got the money to get back on the bus.'

'Alright, jump up.'

I jumped up on one of the horses. I got on his back, no saddle or nothing – blimey, was I sore the next day. We drove those horses right up to the countryside in East Finchley, which I guess must have been seven or eight miles. We let them go in this great big field where he had some kind of stable – not a proper stable, only one that was made up of old wood. I went to take the bridle off his horse.

The old man says, 'Don't stand beside him, stand right in front of him or he'll kick yer brains out.'

As soon as I took the bridle off this horse it stood up on its hind legs and off it went.

This bloke was a costermonger like the Booths. He did some horse dealing, buying working horses to take to Barnet Fair and sell to people for riding. He also sold fruit, vegetables and fish from his barrow on a round. I ended up helping him on Saturdays and Sundays. We would go round the streets in the horse and cart, shout out what we was selling and knock on doors. I got sixpence for helping or, if it was a good week, a shilling or eighteen pence. I helped him on and off for about a year and never knew then that he would turn out to be me father-in-law, Harry Ball.

Mary's father weren't a wealthy man, but he was comfortable cause in the fourteen war he bought horses in for the British Army. He couldn't read or write but he was a very shrewd and careful man who always did business over a half pint of beer – that was all he had usually, no more. When somebody gave him money for a horse he always turned his back to put it away. There was robbing all the time so he always hid his money carefully. He never rolled the notes up in his pocket like some did.

Mary's family was much better off than mine. When I started courting his daughter, her father decided he didn't like me. He knew I was a villain.

We was out one day when she says, 'Me dad don't like you.'

'Oh, don't he!' I says.

'I'm not allowed to see you.'

It didn't make any difference, we carried on seeing each other but I always met her at East Finchley Station or at the Archway, never at her house.

I knew two of Mary's brothers, Harry and Fred, cause they was often at the Archway. I didn't like them much

– Fred was a bully and Harry a cocky sod, he liked hisself. Harry seen me and Mary canoodling in a shop doorway one evening.

'Oi, Cabby,' he says, 'sling yer bleeding hook. Leave my Mary alone.'

I slunk off with me tail between me legs – well, she was his sister and I would have done the same. He went home to tittle tat to his old man.

'She's out with that Cabby Day again.'

That night her father waited for her to come in. He stood in the doorway and when she come in he wiped her round the chops with a rolled up paper – bang! He was a bastard, a proper brute with no mercy for anybody. But it didn't put her off.

Mary was always smart but she could be a proper lad, too. We would walk miles through Parliament Hill Fields and Kenwood and all them places. We liked to go window shopping, or sometimes we would go to the pictures with Chazzer and one of his girlfriends. We went in the ninepennies – that was second class. Sixpence was for the down 'n'outs and the high class was one and thruppence. Sometimes I paid but usually we bunked in. The Palace at Junction Road had back doors and when the film finished they opened them to let the crowd out. As soon as the attendant turned his eyes away, we slipped in and hid in the toilet. Chazzer and me would take the gels in the men's toilet with us, wait a few minutes till the film started, then come out and get into a seat. Me favourite film was *The Big House* with Wallace Beery. It was about some geezers in a prison in America and I seen it about ten times.

We even started going to the Distillery for the weekend entertainment. Mary's parents went there every Sunday night, regular, so we would creep in and get as far away from

them as we could. It was a big place and there was always a
large crowd so they never spotted us.

We liked to go to the fair, too. There was a permanent fair
at the Vale of Health owned by Old Mother Grey. She lived
with her family in a caravan – they was right diddicoys. They
had chair planes that swung you out into the air, roundabouts, coconut shies and a ride called 'Big Bertha'. That was
a ten-foot boat that swung out and back, shaking the life out
of anybody inside. The word went round that a seal had
turned up in the pond at the fair and nobody knew where it
had come from. We went up there to look at it and so did
lots of other people. I reckon Old Mother Grey had got it put
there as a publicity stunt for the fair.

Not long after I started courting Mary, Barnet Fair come
round and we went along. Everyone went there – it was a
river of bodies day and night. Mary looked lovely that day
with her hair right down her back. We was standing watching
the Wall of Death. It was like a deep bowl and the motorbike
rider didn't half have to go to keep the bike at the top of the
rim. After he had been round a few times he rode over to us.
He was black haired and gypsy looking and as brown as a
berry.

'Would you like to ride pillion?' he says to Mary.

I reckon he thought she would look the ticket going round
on the back of his bike with her long yellow hair flying out
in the wind.

'Oh, I don't know,' says Mary.

She was a bit of a daredevil, though.

'What d'you think, Sid?'

'C'mon,' I says, 'show 'em how it's done!'

So she climbed up on the old bike. Attached to the bike
was a sidecar and inside was a tame lion.

'Give him a pat, he won't hurt you,' says the bloke.

The lion was strapped into the sidecar with a collar and harness. He didn't have any teeth so we patted him. He weren't a cub but he weren't full size.

'Right, let's go.'

I stood there petrified watching Mary and the lion fly round the Wall of Death. When the bike come to a halt Mary got off and stood up. She looked frightened out of her life.

'Never again,' she says.

I laughed me head off.

III

Me first car was a Bullnose Morris with a brass radiator to it. It went about forty miles an hour top speed. I shared the car with Chazzer and we repaired it ourselves. There was nothing in repairing those old cars – a farmer could have repaired them with a bit of string. It was just a four cylinder with four plugs. All you had to do was take the head off the engine, clean it out, fit a new set of plugs and away you went again. We kept the Morris on the road outside me house with lights on it at night so people wouldn't fall over it.

I was the only person in the Bay to have a car. There was hardly any cars on the streets – it was mostly horses and carts. Chazzer and me went out in that car but we never had a licence, never had no insurance – nobody bothered about it. We just put the old Guinness label on the front of the car and that was our licence. It was exactly the same colour as the road licence. The colour never altered, always a brown. Me and Chazzer would see the rozzers walking along the roads and holler and laugh at them as we went by.

The cheapest car that was ever made was ninety-nine pounds – it was the Ford Eight. Then there was the little Austin Seven and that was a bit dearer. The police had those in the bigger stations. People had to have a bit of money to have a car, but old bangers could be bought for next door to nothing, say for thirty bob. If you paid ten pound for an old banger it was a good car. I thought nothing of having a car. It was like having a soapbox with two wheels on it to me. Anyone could hire a car for seven and sixpence a day and it would be full up with petrol 'n'all. But most people had no use for a car. They could get all round London for sixpence, and the fare from Highgate to Southend was one and six-pence return. What little bit of money most people earned went on their rent and their feed. They couldn't afford to run motors unless they was on the fiddle.

I sometimes took Mary out in the car and we would go to Southend or to visit her married sister, Sis, at Hornsey. But the main reason I needed a car was for going out and doing villainry of a night time. I got to know a bloke called Ginger who was a steeplejack. Ginger and me drove all over London together. We broke into coffee shops and nicked their one-arm bandits. We took the money out of each machine and sold them on. The Lyons Corner House on Tottenham Court Road was our meeting place for anything like that. There was always somebody to buy the machines from us in there. Everybody you looked at was a crook of some description.

It was a select place, the Lyons Corner House. You felt like one of the high class if you had enough to go in there. They had nice food, served by a nippy with a white apron and a little white hat. It was very, very smart. Ivy Benson's Band played while you ate. There was about ten in her band, all women, and they used to walk round playing their fiddles.

Me favourite meal was prawn salad. It was prawns right the way round a big plate, all peeled off, and lettuce, cucumber and all kinds of salad, chopped up. That was eighteen pence with yer cup of tea. I had that practically every night for supper, sometimes as late as one o'clock in the morning. As long as they had a customer they kept open.

One day I says to Ginger, 'I'll see you in the Corner House tonight.'

'Righto.'

We got talking to these two blokes, brothers, and I sold them one of our machines. I snatched about a fiver off them for it.

They says, 'Any more to come, we'll take all you get.'

Ginger says, 'Yeah, alright.'

As far as I know they put the machines out in clubs and got some blokes who could handle theirselves to look after them. If anyone looked suspicious these blokes would get hold of them by the scruff of their neck and sling them out. It was hard to come by new machines cause they come from America, so they relied on blokes like us to supply them. Sometimes they told us where to go and nick them.

I didn't know who these brothers was but they was important and they knew everybody that was worth knowing. The publicans was scared of them. If they wanted a party in a pub they would say, 'Right, you keep open till we tell you to shut and that's it.' They bribed the police, bribed everybody – you name it, they bribed it. Last I heard of them was when they shot the kneecaps off a bloke in a pub. He had an argument with them and they pulled a gun out and got his knees off.

Ginger and me probably had a hundred or a hundred and fifty machines away in all. One night we went to me brother Bill's garage to get the old Morris. Bill did repairs and sold petrol at his garage, and when he went on holiday I looked after the garage for him. I did little odds and sods for people and would charge them up for it. We cranked up the car and drove up to Bignall's Corner to get petrol. There was a big café there where all the lorries pulled in and filled up with petrol for tenpence a gallon. We pulled up next to a lorry and got out.

'Alright for a tanner a go?' says Ginger to the driver.

'Yeah, fill it up.'

And he says to the attendant, 'Fill that car up as well.'

Then he signed the ticket for the fuel and we paid him sixpence a gallon for our'n. We never bought petrol straight.

That night we nicked two one-arm bandits full of pennies out of coffee shops in Edgware and Burnt Oak. We put them in the back of the car. Then we went to a hotel that we had been told had a new Golden Sovereign machine, brought out to take half a crown. Ginger waited in the car and I went inside. They had the machine in the hallway, right in the middle. I crept up to it and as nobody was about I picked it up and off I went. We got back to the garage, took all the money out of the machines and covered them over with a blanket. Then we went home to bed.

Next morning, I got up and Ginger come for me. We went down the garage and was standing by the car when we seen three blokes walking towards us. I thought to meself, 'Cor blimey, this is the Law,' and it was.

They says, 'Good morning.'

We says, 'Good morning.'

'What have you got covered over there in the back of the car?'

'Some one-arm bandits,' I says.

'Where did you get them from?'

'London Caledonian Market.'

'How much you give for them?'

'Fifty bob each,' says Ginger.

'Hmmm. Lot of money.'

'Yeah, was a lot of money,' I says, 'but they're all good machines.'

They was good machines too, specially the Golden Sovereign.

One of them says, 'We've had enquiries about these machines and we know where they've come from. You'll have to come down the station.'

They took us down the station and charged us with theft. I reckon someone shopped us. Later they altered the charge from theft to receiving stolen property, knowing it to be stolen.

The Law went to me house to confirm that they had me in prison, remanded in custody. The old gel done a drop then. Her and the old man couldn't do anything for me. They didn't know what I had been doing even though I lived at home. After all, they never hardly seen me. Matter of fact somebody once asked me old man what I did for a living and he said, 'Far as I know he's a banana merchant.' And I never sold any bananas, not to that extent anyway.

After a week we went up in front of the judge at the Old Bailey and got seven months' hard labour for each machine – twenty-one months in all, concurrent. They took us to Wormwood Scrubs.

IV

Me dad and me mum come to visit me in prison. They brought Mary with them. Me mum was upset, poor old bugger.

'How are you getting on?' says me mum. 'Do you like it?' Did I like it!

'You silly bastard,' says me dad. 'How did you come to wind up in here?'

Mary didn't say a lot.

'You soppy sod,' says me dad.

It was one man to a cell. Everybody had a Bible and a home-made calendar on the wall for ticking off the days. They come round once a week with books. First thing in the morning was slops out. They would come along, open the door up and holler, 'Slop out, slop out,' all the way down the corridor. We each slopped out, emptying our bucket into the one lavatory on each floor. Didn't it used to stink, Gawd almighty.

Breakfast was porridge and a little loaf of bread, individual cobs weighed out in eight ounces. We had that with a cup of tea – that was our breakfast. They brought it round and we ate it in our cells. Then we had a wash and shave and out we went to do whatever work we was allocated to do. Those who had hard labour broke up these bloody great big kerb stones what was made of granite. They would stay down there all day long in the stone yard with a little hammer going 'bonk, bonk', breaking stones down to chips to put onto the roads. I was stone bashing for a little while but not long.

Whilst I was in the Scrubs they wanted to build a big chimney. Me and some other brickies got the job of putting the foundations in for it. We could only go up about eight foot – they wouldn't let us go any higher. We repaired the slates on the roof of the prison itself, too. They stretched a wire bond from one end of the building to the other. We went up onto the gantry with a big leather belt round us, very thick, with a lock and chain. They locked us to the wire bond and we done our work like that, chained up. It was in case anyone decided to jump off and kill theirselves.

At twelve o'clock we knocked off for an hour dinner break. Our food was rotten – oh, it was terrific in there! Each prisoner had a tin filled up with hot water with a lump of fatty meat slung in. We each also had a cold potato done in its jacket, that was our dinner. The canister weren't tin or anything like that – it was black and dirty looking, bloody awful. The only thing I really enjoyed to eat was a lump of treacle pudding. The pudding was like stone but the treacle was nice and sweet.

After dinner we went out to work again. We couldn't talk when we was working. The only time we could talk was at exercise time. That was diabolical – I hardly ever talked to a soul. We had twenty minutes' exercise twice every day. There was three of us in a row and we all walked round and round in a circle. We couldn't choose who to walk with and so I rarely seen Ginger in all the time I was there.

All the convicts was professionals, or thought they was. All done this and done that and Gawd knows what else. Sometimes, when we was walking round in the circle, someone might say he murdered so and so, but you didn't know much. I got on by keeping meself to meself. That is the only way you can get on in prison. Some people had a hard time. There was a Chinese bloke in there, an opium taker. He would scream, holler and shout but they didn't take any notice.

We knocked off for the day at four o'clock. We weren't allowed to smoke in our cells but we all did. To get a light we would thread some paper on the lead from a pencil and get a light from the electric light fitting. We blew the smoke out the vent that ran up through our cells.

After work they would throw seven or eight mailbags into each cell and we had to make them. They was already cut out and we had to sew them together before lights out at eight o'clock. I was lonely on me own in the cell. It was hard sitting for hours on yer pat when you couldn't read or write, so thank Gawd for the old mailbag making. It kept me brain working and I never had any time to do anything else but go away with the needle and cotton making mailbags. It had to be done – they was strict in there.

The punishment for doing anything wrong was bread and water. I never got bread and water cause I knew I would get a third off me sentence if I behaved meself. After a while they made me a red band, that was for honesty. They gave me the job of drain man and I went about looking after the drains. The red band meant I could walk round the prison without a screw watching me all the time.

The only time they left our doors open was at breakfast and we was supposed to stay in our cells. It all depended what kind of screw you had in charge of you. Every morning they left the porridge churn right outside me door in the middle of the landing. They left it there so they could clear up when we was all finished. While we stood at attention in the doorway they would come round and collect all our dishes before hollering, 'Lock yer doors.'

One morning there was nobody about so I called Ginger over to have a chinwag.

I says, 'Ginger, it's still half full up,' pointing to the churn.

Then he only told the other blokes on the bleeding landing, didn't he. They come up to get more porridge and in the crush they tipped the bleeding lot on the floor of me cell – cor blimey, all that porridge. They was scooping it up and eating it. I thought to meself, 'Bloody hell, if a screw comes in here now he'll hang me.' So I got me bucket of water from the corner of me cell and went down on me hands and knees and washed it all up. I managed to scrub it out before the screws come round.

On visiting days we tidied ourselves up, shaved and used castor oil on our hair. We pressed the crease into our trousers by sleeping on them under the straw mattress the night before. Ruddy come every week to visit me and tell me the news. I looked forward to it. We had half an hour and we all sat on forms – crooks on one side and visitors on the other.

Some of the screws was alright – they was burglars, too.

One says to me one day, 'I want an inch and a quarter brush.'

I says, 'Oh yeah, where am I going to get that?'

He says, 'You're in here for theft, get out and find me one in the stores.'

So I went in the stores and picked up a brush, give it to him and he gave me two Woodbines. I knew he was crooked then.

Next time Mary come to visit I says to her, 'Bring me in a pound note, roll it up tight.'

'Alright, Sid. I will.'

When a visit was over we was allowed to walk down the corridor to the door with our visitors. Mary passed me the rolled-up pound note and I put it in me mouth. The screws knew that trick alright but I had an innocent face.

The next day I seen the crooked screw in the stoke house.

I says, 'I've got a nicker here. Can you spend it for me?'

He says, 'Yeah alright, half whack.'

So I give him the pound note and he brought me in ten shillings' worth of gear. He got me some boiled eggs for eighteen pence each, some chocolates, razor blades, cigarettes and sweets, but he never give them to me. He told me to look in the stoke house amongst the coke and I found them there. At the death I was spending other people's money with him. A bloke would give twenty bob and get five bob's worth of gear. The screw had ten bob and my cut was five bob.

V

When I got out of the Scrubs I carried on courting Mary, if you could call it courting. Oh dear, the times I let poor old Mary down and left her waiting for me at the station. When you had a girlfriend you was supposed to see them nearly every evening. I would do that for a while, then it would go to three times a week, then I might go a month without seeing her. I would bump into her at the Archway and she would say, 'Where have you been?' And I would say, 'I've been very busy getting me living.' Then we would go and have a coffee and I would arrange to see her again.

Mary had three sisters but she was the prettiest and she had lots of admirers. There was a hairdresser, who had two or three shops, wanted to take her out but she wouldn't wear it. She was in love with me. I took her round to visit me mother one day. We had tea and rock cakes. When we got up to leave me mum started laughing.

'You'll know you've got him when you've got him,' she says to Mary.

I had never wanted to get married and have kids cause I always thought it weren't a fit world to bring kids into really. But when me mum said that about settling down – well, I thought to meself, 'I'm twenty-three, I might just as well get married.'

Things was very hard at the time so I had to borrow half a crown off Mary to pay the licence fee. I only had five shillings and it was seven and sixpence. Most wedding receptions was held in pubs. The guests went straight to the pub after the registry office and all got drunk. But our wedding was held at Mary's house and did we have a big party! Me mates Ruddy, Cocker, Ginger, Chazzer, our parents and some of our brothers and sisters come to the do. She wore a two-piece with a rabbit fur trim in her favourite colour, green. She had a gold wedding ring with platinum inside that cost six quid.

Mary's old man owned his own property and always had plenty of money. But he was that bleeding tight he wouldn't throw his shit to the crows. He was supposed to supply all the salad stuff for the wedding tea but the rotten old bastard charged us for it. Mary's mother didn't say anything against it. She was a proper costermonger's wife – looked more like a gypsy than anything else – and her husband was the law in the household. Still, there was a big crowd there and we had a good booze up and I got as drunk as a lord. The next morning I went straight to bleeding work.

Our first home was in Muswell Hill for twelve and sixpence a week – two rooms and a shared bathroom. It was easy to get flats but it was hard affording the rent. I also wanted to set up a proper home for us with new furniture. There was a shop in Brixton called Hardy's that sold very nice furniture. They had a bedroom suite in maple bird's eye. Boy, it was a pretty suite. They also had a great big double wardrobe and a single wardrobe and a bed.

I says to the owner, 'I want that and that and that. How much a week have I got to pay for that lot?'

He got the old pencil and paper out.

'Three and a tanner a week.'

I says, 'What's the total come to then?'

'Fifty-seven pounds for the whole lot.'

'Yep, that's alright, I'll have it.'

Before I got married I had only meself to keep and no home to pay for. Mary was working in a glass-blowing factory and I was a jobbing builder, but we still had a hard job paying for everything and we never had anything to spare. We was that poor that one day Mary never had enough to buy a pennorth of dripping to fill the fat pan to cook chips for our dinner. So she topped up the pan with some water and nearly set herself alight, the silly mare.

Mary had a good education and always spoke her mind about what she didn't like. Even though I was a married man I carried on like before for a little while. One night me mates come up in the car.

'C'mon, Cabby,' says Chazzer. 'We're going to Southend.'

So I says to Mary, 'I won't be long, I'm popping down to Southend.'

But she didn't like it and cor, didn't she cry when I come back – poor old Mary.

The next night when I got home from work she marched on about it again. We had a big row and I ended up saying, 'Well, sling yer bleeding hook out of it.' She left the house crying. After a while I felt sorry and thought to meself, 'Where the bleeding hell has she gone, I'll go out for a walk and see if I can find her.' I found her in Cherry Tree Wood, sitting on a park bench.

I says, 'What are you doing out here? C'mon home.'

After that I thought to meself, 'Aw, sod that lark, it's time I packed up.' So I packed up going out with me mates and going out thieving and Gawd knows what else. It was difficult cause I was used to going where I liked, when I liked and how I liked. But Mary was pregnant and I decided to knuckle down.

Three months after we got married Ruddy got married to Jess. She was a pretty gel. They had a boy and a gel and Ruddy quietened down. The gel went into the police force when she grew up. When Bootnose packed up at the billiard hall Ruddy become the manager. As far as I know it was the first proper job he had.

Chazzer got married, too. He picked up a tart in the Bay name of Nancy America. She was nineteen, tall, slim and very pretty with long dark hair. He chatted her up and they had a bunk up and she got pregnant. I was in Gayler's with him and Ruddy when he told us.

'I've got me tart in the family way,' says Chazzer.

'Oh,' says Ruddy.

'I don't know whether to get married to her or not,' he says. We just laughed.

'You would laugh you bastards, wouldn't you!'

When a bloke got a gel pregnant he either married her or lived with her. Sometimes the bloke stayed, sometimes he didn't. The women just had to get on with it. One bloke I knew had kids with the woman he lived with and she was never without a black eye. He was a bastard, always coming home drunk and setting about her. Some blokes treated women like bloody slaves, there's no doubt about it. Lots of blokes cheated on their wives. Cocker and me did some work for a woman in Junction Road who thought her husband had someone else.

One day she says to us, 'Will you tail him for me if I give you eighteen pence to cover yer fares?'

Cocker and I thought it would be a lark.

'Alright,' we says.

'Please make a note of what he does and where he goes.'

I thought to meself, 'What a pair of sparks to send out as detectives when neither of us can read or write.' But off we went after her husband. He got on a bus, we got on a bus. He got on a tram, we got on a tram. We followed him through Kentish Town to Camden Town till he went inside a house. We couldn't read the road name so we didn't know where the hell we was.

'Oh, let's keep out of it,' says Cocker.

So we kept the rest of the eighteen pence and forgot all about him.

Chazzer left it till the last minute to marry Nancy. I think they had about four or five kids before he wound up a wino. Me words come right. When I was working down Highbury after the war I stopped for lunch in the playing field just outside the town. I was eating me sandwiches when a bloke come into sight, wobbling along. I thought to meself, 'I know that bloke from somewhere.' It was Chazzer.

I shouts, 'Oi, Chazzer.'

'Who're you oi-ing?'

I says, 'You – you're Chazzer, ain't yer?'

'Who are you then?' he asks.

'I'm Cabby.'

'Hang me! Fancy seeing you here.'

I talked to him for a few minutes but he weren't making no sense. It was only midday and he was well drunk.

'Oh, you've gone way over the top you have, mate,' I says.

And off he went on his way. I never see him again.

Mary

VI

I started working all hours to try and get ahead in life. I worked for a guvnor and worked for meself. I worked on the underpinning of the British Museum where it was giving way. I worked at the Isle of Dogs where the Scandinavians and the Laskars come over on boats with crates of chickens. I worked for firms, but it paid better to work for meself when I could.

There was plenty of Irish in the building. When there was no work there was hundreds of Irish undercutting our blokes by walking round with placards saying, 'Three labourers for half a crown an hour'. In some places jobs was meant to go for local people only – but the Irish slept in the kip houses till they qualified as locals. Sometimes the hounds would set about the Irish for going for our jobs, but on site we got on alright. All they thought about was women and booze, but they worked hard.

I knew a bloke called McGinty who was the mixer driver at a site where me brother Bill was foreman. I was dibbing in and out of there – Bill let me go off and do me own work when I had some. McGinty was a hell of a strong man. We was building council flats and one day I see him carry a concrete lintel up a ladder that must have weighed two hundredweight and a half. He was in the pub till ten at night and when they turned him out he would creep back and sleep in the cement shed. He had been a farmer in Ireland and come over cause they never earned no money, poor sods. At Christmas he would go home and he always sent Bill a turkey or a goose to make sure he kept his job.

Mary carried on working till the baby was born. It nearly arrived in the cab to the hospital. I had to get angry with the driver and make him go through the lights. When we got to the hospital Mary went in and I never seen her or the baby till the next week on visiting day. That was the first time they would let me in.

When I went in Mary says, 'What do you think?'

I looked at the little baby.

'She looks like a baby rabbit,' I says.

'You cheeky sod!' says Mary.

The baby come home and we decided to name her Shirley Ann and have a christening party. We liked to go window shopping and we had seen a baby piano in the window of Hardy's in the same wood as our bedroom suite.

I says to Mary, 'We'll have that piano.'

She says, 'We got no money for pianos.'

'Don't matter, we'll have it.'

And I went in and got it. We had the christening party, kept it for about six months and then sent it back.

Not long after Shirley was born we heard that Sis was ill. Sis was Mary's favourite sister and she never missed seeing her and the kids regular. She sometimes took some potatoes or fruit pinched from her father's shop to help them out. Sis's husband was a plasterer but he was a lazy bastard and a drinker – he hardly ever worked. They was as poor as church mice. Sis was in bed ill for days and she just got worse and worse. When I went in to see her she was on her last knockings. Her belly was all bloated out. In the end they took her into hospital where she died.

Sis weren't even thirty years old when she went and she left three children. It weren't till a long while after that I found out what happened to her. She was pregnant and couldn't see how they could afford another baby – they could hardly keep the ones they had. So she had a back street abortion and it killed her.

We had the two gels to live with us for a while. The boy stayed with his father's family. They slept on a bed in our sitting room and one of them wet the bed every night. It was drownded every morning. She was only five or six years old, poor little mite. It all got on top of Mary and after a few months one of his sisters took them. When their father got married again he had them back, but they had a hell of a life. Mary never had a good word to say about him, but she always kept in touch with the gels and they come round from time to time. The eldest married a black bloke and moved to New Zealand. We never found out he was black till the day of the wedding.

When Sis's gels had gone and Shirley was still a little teeny baby, we moved to live with me brother Jim and his wife Min out at Kingston. We rented a big bungalow there – a butterfly bungalow, two wings and a body. They had three quarters of it, cause they had lots of kids, and we had a quarter. There was plenty of land round the bungalow so we kept about a dozen goats and some chickens.

We had two cars – I think I give five pound for the two – and me and Jim would go to work at Peckham in one or other of them. It would take about half an hour to crank up a car and get the bleeding thing going in the mornings. Going along Peckham High Road there was tram lines. The first time we went out I was going too fast and I got me wheels stuck in one of them. I was heading straight for a crowd waiting for the tram. I didn't know what to do so I went up on the pavement, round the crowd, and back down again.

Jim says, 'This is the last bleeding time I go out with you!'

A few weeks later we was on Blackfriars Bridge when the bloody thing stalled. A policeman come up.

He says, 'What's the matter?'

I says, 'It just stalled.'

'I see you got L-plates on. Are you a driver?'

I says, 'Yeah. He's the passenger, I'm teaching him to drive.'

'Oh, you're the instructor.'

'Yeah.'

'Well, best of luck to you.'

He never asked if I had a licence or anything. Bleeding good job cause I never had no licence, no insurance, bugger all.

We moved from Kingston to Leicester Road in East Finchley, near to Mary's family. I carried on as a builder but I bought a removals lorry for a sideline. Mary worked too – she was a very hard worker, too hard working for her own good. When she had finished her own work she would clean the house for her parents – they expected it. She started working for the Co-op in the chemist department. Everybody belonged to the Co-op then cause they give their customers sixpence in the pound. Each stamp on yer card was worth sixpence and come Christmas time you probably had a few pounds saved.

Every morning we took Shirley to me sister Lou's house in Hornsey. We paid Lou to look after her so we could work. Shirley was a little perisher – I had to carry her everywhere. After doing a day's work, laying a thousand bricks in a day, I had to carry that little gel right across Alexandra Park up to the top of the hill. She wouldn't walk a bleeding step.

After work Cocker was always at our house. Mary didn't like me other mates but she was very fond of Cocker. He and his brother Bert was mad on the greyhound racing.

One day he says to us, 'Are you coming to Hendon to the dogs with us?'

'Not likely,' I says. 'We haven't got any bleeding money for dogs.'

He says, 'C'mon, I'll pay yer grey mare.'

I says to Mary, 'What do you think?'

'Yeah, I'd like to, George.'

So down to Hendon we went and Cocker told us which dogs had a chance and which had no chance. At the finish I won sixteen pounds and Cocker won a few pounds, too. After that I went several more times with him till I lost a fiver. Then I thought to meself, 'I ain't standing for that lark,' and I never went any more. George still went regular every week. If he had a good win he would come round and say to Mary, 'Here you are, Mary, put it in yer outer.' He liked to treat Mary and Shirley. Shirley loved to sit on his lap and comb his hair – he had plenty of lovely black hair greased back from his forehead with Brylcreem. She would part it in the middle and comb it down both sides and we would all laugh our socks off.

Cocker was a loner. Sometimes you couldn't get anything out of him, he shut up like a clam. His left arm never knew what his right arm was doing. I called him Silent George. But he was a generous man. If he had a shilling he would give you sixpence – he would give his heart away. We liked to go out for trips in the car together. Cocker, Mary, me and the baby went to Southend for the day in me red van. Coming home two blokes in a car edged me onto the pavement at the crossroads cause there was a traffic jam.

I says, 'The bastards, they could have killed us.'

'Tail them home,' says Cocker.

They pulled into a pub. We got out of the van and went up to them. Cocker hit one and knocked him out and I hit the other one. Then we left. We hadn't been indoors ten minutes when the police knocked on the door.

'Was you at the Cambridge public house? Did you hit two men?'

'Yeah, they drove into us on the road and we punished them.'

'What did you use?'

'Fists.'

'Show us yer hands.' We did.

One of them says to Cocker, 'Sure you never had a knuckle duster on?'

Cocker was very gentle for such a big, strong man, but he had a temper and sometimes it got the better of him.

PART FOUR

I

Chamberlain come back from Germany and stood there holding a piece of paper up in the air saying, 'Peace in our time.' Not long afterwards we was at war.

The war was announced on the radio in the morning. The announcer said, 'This country is now at war with Germany,' and I think they sounded the sirens. I was working on a site that employed mainly Irishmen. Directly after the radio announcement all these Irishmen slung their shovels and their hods up in the air and scooted off back to Ireland. They just packed up and went home.

In the evening Jean was born. I will always remember the midwife coming out to tell me. I was sitting in the kitchen, waiting. She come in smiling.

She says, 'You must come in and see yer lovely little rosebud.'

I went in the bedroom to see Jean and she was a little rosebud, no ifs and buts about it. That midwife thought the world of that little gel. She come every day to see her and Mary.

We was living in Leicester Road and I had a rented yard off Manor Road with a shed and pigsties where I kept me gear.

As we was only about five doors away from Mary's father and mother, I says to the old man, 'What about having Mary up in yer house so I can go to work?'

'Yes, alright,' he says.

'Righto. I'll get a pair of steps and we'll put some pillows on it and make a stretcher of it.'

So I carried her up to her father's house and she slept in the front room. She was in bed for the first ten days of the war.

We was like everybody else, just wondering what was going to happen to us. They said Hitler might capitulate but he went forward. We all thought the Germans would invade us. I thought to meself, 'There's only that little drop of water there to stop them coming over.' But if the Germans had walked up our street it would have just been a matter of 'Right, we're the top dogs now.' Our lives would have gone on just the same.

People was saying, 'If it weren't for the Jews we wouldn't have a war.' They said the Jews was taking over the world and that was why Hitler was against them. It was nothing to me – I did lots of work for Jews round Hampstead. Matter of fact, I was working for this Jewish woman during the war when three of her brothers arrived after escaping from a prison camp. The old gel called me over one day.

She says, 'Have a look at that, Sid – there you are, there's his number on there.'

One of them showed me the numbers printed on their wrist. I felt sorry for them, though they couldn't speak a word of bloody English. I thought they was escaped prisoners of war. We didn't know about the gassing till near the end of the war when our soldiers went into the camps.

When the war was announced I decided to do me duty for King and country and volunteer for the Navy. We didn't think it would go on for more than a few months. Me dad would always say, 'If you go in the services join the Navy and see the world.' I went down to the drill hall at Burnt Oak to sign up. When I got there they took about twenty of us inside where some desks and chairs was set up like a classroom. They put a paper in front of each of us. I thought to meself, 'I can't fill that in,' so I left it blank. Then a bloke took them all in and marched us out.

After a while we was taken back inside. They had shifted it all round and there was three tables – one for the Army, one for the Air Force and one for the Navy. I went up to the Navy bloke – he had gold all round his hat and up his arms.

He says, 'You want to go in the Navy?'

'Yes, sir.'

'What's your name?'

'Sidney Thomas Day.'

He looked for me papers but I told him that I couldn't fill in the form.

'Oh, well, sorry, your education isn't up to standard then,' he says.

'Eh! I ain't got to write home and tell me old woman that I'm stoking the fires up.'

'Over there,' he says crossly. 'Under the clock!'

The Air Force table was under the clock. I went over and got in the line. The bloke there took all me particulars.

'Rear gunner, you,' he says.

'What!'

I didn't want none of that lark.

'Yes, you'll make a good rear gunner.'

'Will I? I ain't doing that. Where can I sign on as a conscientious objector?'

He looked at me as if I had gone bleeding mad. Then he opened the drawer and pulled some papers out.

'Yes, alright, you can do it here,' he says.

So I signed on as a conchie.

Building was made a reserved occupation so that shelters could get built. I got a letter telling me I was in the Hornsey Borough Council ARP, based in Fortis Green. Our first job was to build air raid shelters on the corners of the roads. Each shelter was meant for several families and was built of eighteen-inch brickwork with a concrete roof and one doorway. They was about eight foot high and looked like a low warehouse.

Everything went quiet for months and months. We wondered what was going to happen – we all talked about it. We never heard nothing, never seen nothing for months. Night and day everything was quiet. There was no traffic cause you had to have a government job to get petrol. I could get it cause I was doing shelters, but I was only allocated two gallons a week.

One night just after the war started, Mary and me went to the pictures. Coming out we went past Jerome's, a little jewellery shop. We stopped and looked in the window and I seen a lovely ring there.

I says to Mary, 'Would you like a ring like that?'

'Oh yeah, I would.'

'C'mon then. Let's go in and buy it.'

In the shop we goes. The little old boy in charge had a club foot.

I says, 'We want to buy a ring, mate.'

'Oh yes. What sort of ring you looking for?'

'You got one in the window there with three stones in it.'

'I'll get the tray out for you.'

He got the tray out full of rings and put it on the glass top counter. Just as he started laying the rings out the sirens went. It was the first air raid warning. At that time nobody knew what might happen so the old boy panicked. He started to scoop the rings up back into the tray.

'Out you go, out you go,' he says. 'I must get to the shelter.'

'We'll come back later on then.'

'Come back tomorrow, come back tomorrow.'

'Righto. We will.'

When we gets up the road and away from the shop, I turned to Mary.

'There you go, mate, there's the ring you was looking for,' I says.

And I took the ring out of me mouth and put it onto her finger.

'You bleeding monkey,' she says.

When the air raids started it was our job in the ARP to pull people out from under the rubble, prop up houses and make them safe, see to things what was dangerous and clear up. I got three pounds ten a week and worked a twelve-hour shift – either during the day or night – but we was on call twenty-four hours a day. On night shift we stayed at the depot in bunk beds and played cards till we went to sleep. We got up in the morning when it was all quiet, made our beds and went home about eight o'clock. Then another shift would come on.

I took on the job of cook, cause nobody else wanted to do it and I could see the perks. When I was doing the cooking I would get on the dirty tyke about ten o'clock at night and fetch about ten pound of sugar home. I also made apple tarts and put them in the bushes in the front garden for Mary to collect in the morning. All sorts of eating stuff I would bring home.

I cooked for about sixty men. They had a proper dinner – roast lamb, roast beef or chicken with apple and custard for pudding. One day they wanted spotted dick for their afters and so I made this spotted dick. It was like the bleeding rocks of Gibraltar. They couldn't eat the thing – it was too hard for them to get their chops round. So I asked Mary, 'How do you make the spotted dick?' She told me the mixtures. After that I was alright and I could make it for them whenever they wanted.

The first bomb I knew about fell at Hornsey. The German bombers dropped several others that night, too. At about ten o'clock the red light went up in our shed. I was in the cook-house making tea and one of the blokes come to get me.

'There's a bomb hit Hornsey and knocked down two houses,' he says.

We all jumped in the lorry and went up there. We pulled out two dead women from underneath the rubble. I seen many a dead person over on the heath drownded in the water so I knew what to expect. Me and one of the other blokes looked at these bodies. I could see him looking at the rings they was wearing, nice rings, worth money. He took them off their fingers.

I says, 'I'll give you ten pounds for those if you don't want to hand them in, mate.'

'Alright,' he says.

I took them back to Mary and told her I had found them in the rubble.

The next day I went into the depot and this bloke come hurrying up to me.

'Sid,' he says. 'Here's yer ten pound back. You've got to give me those rings. I ain't slept a wink all night.'

Sid (bottom left) as foreman of his ARP unit.

II

Once it got started the bombing went on every night of the week – it never stopped. The planes come and dropped their bombs and we had to stick brown paper on the windows to stop the glass shattering. I dug a big hole in our garden for a corrugated iron Anderson shelter and buried it in the ground. The top of it was ground level and we had a mattress down there and a stove for making a cup of tea. I had it done out nicely, concreted all round the sides. When the concrete let through the damp I nicked some asphalt and melted it in a dustbin to put on the walls. Mary handed it down to me in buckets – it was like tar and very messy. We really sweated doing that job but it did the trick.

Mary and the kids went into the shelter every night but she hated it. I was out most nights with the ARP. I ended up as foreman and I had twelve men and a lorry with big shovels and hydraulic lifts, and Gawd knows what else in it. The bombing was never ending. There was another terrific raid on Hornsey that flattened dozens of houses.

A fortnight later we was still down there shoring up houses. It was daybreak when I see a plane come out of the clouds.

I says to one of me blokes, 'Look, there's a bleeding German plane up there.'

'Yeah, there is,' he says.

I followed it with me eyes and thought to meself, 'Cor blimey, he's going towards East Finchley.' The bomb went out and away and went bang.

'That bleeding bomb is near me house,' I says.

'No, no it can't be, mate.'

I tore home and the bomb had dropped at the end of the road and knocked the sweet shop out. All the windows in me house and other houses all round was broken. It knocked out about thirty shops altogether up on the main road. Mary, the gels and our neighbour, Mrs Hicks, was in the shelter. They was shook up but alright.

At night time everything was blacked out. The warden come round every night and if he could see a strip or a pin hole of light he would knock on the door and say, 'You've got a light shining there, seal it up.' From Leicester Road we could see the flash from Big Bertha hidden in the railway tunnel that ran through Highgate Wood. The gunner sat in that tunnel and all of a sudden he would pop out and – bang

– off would go his big gun and shatter everything round him. Then he would go back in till the next time.

People took no notice of the air raids at the finish. The pubs used to be crowded out every night. All the women and men was drunk and you had to claw yer way through the smoke. They was all smoking away and singing and if the sirens went off they just stopped in there.

So life went on as usual. I got friendly with this Leo who lived up the road over Mary's brother Fred's shop. Leo was a signwriter – I met him when he was about to start work painting up Fred's name over the shop.

'I want something a bit different to everyone else,' says Fred.

'How about yer name in bananas?' I says.

'Good idea,' says Leo.

So he made all the letters look like bananas. After that me and Mary would go out for a drink with him and his wife, Lil.

Leo got ill with an ulcerated stomach and he was bedridden for quite some time. He and Lil had three or four kids so it was hard for them and they had the rent to pay. Leo knew some bloke who had a factory in New Barnet that made umbrellas. It got closed down when the war started but it was full of brolly bits and pieces. Leo asked me to go up and see this bloke for him and bring back some handles.

'What do you want them for?' I says.

'Making ashtrays, Sid,' he says.

The handles was made of some kind of bone or ivory and he attached them to bowls to make the ashtrays. The handle was for resting the cigarette on. He also made cufflinks out of mother of pearl buttons. When I was at home I would help Mary for a while with the leather bags that she made and then I might go up to see Leo for a chinwag and help

him make ashtrays. That was how he got by till he was able
to work again.

One day he says, 'Do you want to use the car, Sid – take
the family out for the day?'

'Yes, I think I will, Leo. I've got a bit of petrol from me
ARP allowance,' I says.

I killed a chicken and Mary roasted it till it was all golden
and beautiful and she cooked some potatoes and peas. We
packed the lot in a basket and went to Southend for the day.
We was sitting on the beach looking at the sea and all the
war defences. Everyone was looking at our food thinking,
'They must be millionaires to have food like that!' After a
good nosh up we got back in the car to go back home. Halfway back there was a crash and a wallop and the battery fell
out of the car and onto the road. I had a hell of a job getting
it back in again.

Not long after our outing we had to take in some lodgers.
The authorities come round to ask if we could put up some
Polish evacuees till they got accommodation. So we took in
a woman and her daughter. They didn't like us and they was
right know-alls. I think they resented the English people for
some reason. The old gel would sit by the fire at night and
spit into it, dirty cow – so we never kept them long.

After they had gone, Cocker turned up, on leave from the
Army. He was stationed in the Orkneys.

Mary says, 'How's the Army?'

'Sod the Army – it's too bleeding cold up there,' he says.

'You going to blow then, George?' I says.

'You can kip here if you do,' says Mary.

So Cocker never went back. He had no fear about trotting
and they never caught up with him. He stopped with us for
a while but couldn't get a job cause he didn't have cards. In
the end I taught him how to lay bricks and he went black-

legging. He come and went but we never knew what he was up to or where he was till he turned up. George was a silent night.

Cocker and me took on a private job for a bloke name of Knight in Totteridge – we done the drainage for his pigsties. Near the end of the job he come out to feed his pigs.

I says to Knight, 'Arthur, what about a bit of pork?'

'Yeah, alright then. How much do you want?'

'Well, I got a big family.'

He says, 'What about that one over there?' He pointed to a middling size pig.

'Yeah, he'll do.'

He got the gun and shot him right there – over he went. Then he slit him down, gutted him and dipped him in boiling water. All the pig's hair come off in the water, then he was hung up on a hook. The next day I went to collect him.

'Yer meat's ready,' says Knight.

'How much I got to give you for it?'

'That's alright,' he says.

On the way home I says to Cocker, 'We'll have roast pork every day of the week.'

Mary couldn't believe her eyes. We cut the pig up as best we could and stashed all the meat in our fridge. The next morning we come downstairs and there was a smell of burning. It was coming from the fridge. Inside was a light made of Bakelite and it had melted onto the meat.

We cooked up some of the meat but it was all tainted with the smell.

'Oh, Sid – what you going to do now?' says Mary.

We tried every way of cooking it to get rid of that taste but it was still there. I took it to the butcher's and asked them to salt it but it was no good. In the end I had to cook it and feed it to the chickens.

As well as keeping rabbits, ducks and chickens in the
garden I had vegetables on me allotment. Everyone grew
something, even if it was in their back garden. I grew plenty
of onions. They wasn't on ration but you just couldn't find
them in the shops. When you found them you was lucky. I
would give some of the ones I grew to Mrs Hicks, the old gel
who lived next door to us. She was a big, fat woman and she
had four sons and two daughters. Talk about lovely looking
boys, cor blimey – the eldest was a pilot in the Air Force. He
was about six feet two and was he a smart bloke!

Mrs Hicks was the best forager going. We would be in the
house and all of a sudden we would hear – bang – something
hit the back door. When we opened the back door Mrs Hicks
would say, 'Day, there's a lump of soap there for you.' Or it
would be a lump of butter. She was a marvellous old gel, the
way she got round those shopkeepers. She would come running in mid-morning and say, 'Mary, they got so and so up the
road, get up there before it's all gone.' Mary would put her
skates on and up she would go. It might be fish or something
like that. We only got the bare necessities on ration, like
sugar, butter, meat and clothes. There was no such thing as
fruit or bananas in the shops, though if you had the money
you could get anything you wanted on the black market.
There was always somebody with something to sell.

III

A mate of mine, Blackie, never sold anything straight. I would
say to him, 'Blackie, what about a piece of bacon or some
butter?' 'Leave it to me, Sidney,' he would say. Blackie was

always round at our house. I first met him years before I got married, when I lived in the Bay. I bumped into him fishing on Hampstead Heath and we got talking. He lived in a posh part of Highgate and his father worked for Sotheby's as a porter. He always had money in his pocket and so I would tap him up. I would wait for him at the end of the alleyway into our road and say, 'Lend us a tanner, Blackie.' In the end he started taking the long way round in case I was waiting for him. Still, for some reason he thought the world of me and Mary.

Before the war Blackie worked for Dunn's the hatmakers. He was always a smart man, in his Savile Row clothes. When he left there he bought a motorbike and took sandwiches to the rag trade sweatshops, where he sold them to the Jewish workers. It was there that he met a maker who asked him if he could sell any 'cabbage' – that was the name for an extra two lengths they could get out of a roll meant for twenty dresses. So he started dealing in cloth and women's dresses. One day he brought some dresses round.

'Oh, Sidney,' he says, 'is Mary here? I've got some beautiful dresses.'

'How much?'

'Seven and sixpence,' he says, and showed me the clothes.

'Five bob's plenty,' I says. I always refused his asking price.

'Oh, Sidney, let me live! It's got to be seven and sixpence.'

And he would wave his hands in that Yiddish way he had picked up from his customers in the East End. We always said he should have been Jewish and that's why he got on so well with them.

'Five bob's yer lot.'

Blackie would go from Finchley to Barnet to make a penny profit on half a dozen eggs. Through the whole war he was running round on that bike, buying and selling – you name it, he sold it. He picked up some old tart and married her, but she left him in the end cause he was never at home – he was always off somewhere on his bike. He ended up with his own ladies' clothing business at Holloway on Seven Sisters Road.

The real king of the black market, though, was a bloke name of Joby Finch. This Joby even used to serve a policeman at the station in Fortis Green. He often paid me to deliver a hundredweight of black market corn to him for his chickens – everybody kept chickens. Both me and Joby was regulars at the Black Bess Café in East Finchley. One day I was having a cup of tea when Joby come in.

'Ah, Sid,' he says. 'Got anything on this afternoon?'

'No – why?'

'Can you do me a favour and cart eight pigs in yer lorry? I want to take them over to Tottenham.'

I did a lot of carting for people in me lorry.

I says, 'You know I'm not allowed to take bloody pigs in the lorry, I ain't got a licence.'

'You ain't got a licence to do a lot of things. What about it? I'll pay you well.'

'What do you call well?'

'I'll give you fifteen nicker.'

'Righto,' I says, 'I'll be there. Whereabouts?'

'Down by the Green Man.'

'What time do you want me there?'

'I want you there bang on twelve o'clock, if you can make it.'

When I got there Joby and another bloke was standing at the gate.

Joby says, 'Back round, Sid – back yer wagon round, drop the tail down.'

I backed round and they opened the gate and whooshed

the pigs in. I took these pigs down to Tottenham into a piggery and he give me the fifteen pounds. What I didn't know was that they was nicking them. If I had got caught I could have got twenty bloody years! But I didn't know the whole thing was crooked till about twelve months afterwards.

Joby lived near me mate – a plumber who had done some work with me. He told me that Joby had a stable for keeping the horses he bought and sold. The stable was opposite an RSPCA place where they took in animals. When I found out about the pigs I thought to meself, 'I'll have me own back with you, you bastard,' and I waited up there. I waited in the RSPCA yard till I seen him take in some crooked gear, two boxes. He come out, locked the doors and off he went. Then I went to the stable and put the iron in the door. Whoop – the door opened and I had away two boxes of his cigarettes.

During the war there weren't a person breathed that said, 'I mustn't have that. I must live on me rations like I am supposed to do.' I was in the Black Bess one dinnertime when I heard the owner, Sid, talking to this geezer called Steve – a lorry driver who carted stuff to and from the railway.

'Can't you get me a bit of gear,' says Sid to Steve.

'Well, I often do get stuff and I don't know where to plant it,' says Steve.

'Well, you can plant it here.'

After that I watched Steve come in with parcels of this and that for Sid. He brought in a board and pencil and Sid signed for each parcel so it looked official. Old Sid did well out of it. He weren't a wealthy man but he had a bit put away. In fact he told me he had some savings in a tin down a manhole near where he lived in Hertfordshire. I thought to meself, 'I'll get in on that game.' So I got in with this Steve and he supplied me with all sorts of stuff during the war, like rolls of cloth and cigarettes. Once I had a big box of women's shoes off of him. Everyone knows a woman is the worst person to sell anything to in the clothing department, and no matter who I tried there was nothing to suit. I don't think I sold one pair of those shoes and I had to give them away at the death.

Freddie and Joey Booth was all over London selling crooked gear during the war. They went into the Black Bess one day.

Freddie says to Sid, 'We've got three boxes of John Player's cigarettes. Do you want to buy them?'

'How much?'

'No messing round. We'll take a hundred pound for the lot.'

They had a sample of what they was going to sell and they showed it to Sid. They said they had got them off the railway.

'Back yer lorry down here then – in the gates and unload them.'

They unloaded about three cases of cigarettes all done up as if they was straight from the factory. Sid coughed up his hundred pounds and off they went. When he opened the cases up all he had was celery tops. The Booths had put all that rotten old stuff into the boxes and sold them to poor Sid.

Another trick they had was to get hold of used whisky bottles and re-label them. Then they made tea and watered it down till they got it to the colour of whisky. They run this cold tea through blotting paper into the bottles so it ran clear and then they sold it. They took some bottles to the big café on Bignall's Corner. Freddie went in to see the owner with a proper bottle of scotch.

He says, 'Can you do with any of that, mate?'

'How many you got?'

'Oh, about a hundred and fifty bottles.'

'Cor blimey, I don't want all that.'

'Well, you can have a hundred pounds' worth, if you want it.'

The bloke coughed up but all he got was bottles of cold tea for his whisky. He weren't supposed to be buying crooked whisky so there was nothing he could do about it.

IV

Christmas come and I seen some turkeys in the window of the butcher's shop on the High Road. I thought to meself, 'Blimey, there's some lovely turkeys, I'll have one of those tonight.' During the air raids shops didn't bother getting their windows repaired, but sealed them up with hardboard leaving a small square of glass in the middle so you could look inside. It was easy to break through them. When it got dark I went up there and made a hole in the window to hook out a turkey. I put me head in but there weren't a bleeding thing in there! All the turkeys was back in the fridge.

As I walked home I see a purse on the road. I picked it up and had a look in it. There was one pound fifteen and sixpence inside. I thought to meself, 'Here's some poor old bugger's purse, Christmas time 'n'all.' There was nobody about so I put it in me bin and took it home.

I says to Mary, 'I just picked this up off the road, should I hand it in to the nick?'

She thought about it.

Then she says, 'Yes, you better, it might be somebody's Christmas dinner.'

I was pretty skint and it did cross me mind to keep it. It was a big temptation, but I thought to meself, 'It might be somebody with two or three kiddies and no Christmas dinner.' So I took it up the police station at Fortis Green. A copper was behind the desk.

'I found this outside the butcher's on East Finchley High Road.'

'Oh yeah,' he says.

He got out his ledger and wrote down me name and address.

'Come back in three months' time,' he says. 'If it's not claimed you can have it.'

That same Christmas I was out with Cocker in the lorry seeing what we could nick. We was going down this country lane when I seen this beautiful tree of holly, absolutely smothered with berries.

I says, 'George, we'll have that. We'll have him over on the way back.'

On the way back we stopped the lorry right underneath the tree and got out and started cutting the holly. Two blokes come up with guns.

'What are you doing?'

I says, 'Cutting some holly.'

One says, 'Who's given you permission to take it?'

'Mr Sparrow at that farm over there.'

'No Mr Sparrow lives there. It's my holly and you've got no right to it.'

'Well,' I says, 'I'm awfully sorry but I'm prepared to pay you for it if I've done any damage.'

'You're prepared to pay?'

'Oh yes, if I've done wrong, I'll pay.'

'Right then. Go down to the bottom of the road, turn left, go in the white gates and wait there.'

We went to his farm house and he took us inside.

'Now, how much do you reckon that tree's worth to you?'

I says, 'Oh, I don't know, guvnor, a couple of quid?'

He says, 'Two quid! That's not a lot of money for holly like that.'

'Well, we've got to sell it and we've got to cut it down,' I says.

'Make a cup of tea,' he says to his wife.

We had a cup of tea and sat down and talked about the farm.

'Well,' he says, 'you seem like an honest man to me – and genuine. There's three trees on the farm, take what you want off them but don't damage the trees. We don't want yer two quid.'

When we got outside I says to Cocker, 'Has he gone bleeding mad?'

We went and stripped the trees, took the holly home and sold it for a nice profit.

A few years later, in the freeze-up of 1947, when nobody and nothing could move for snow and ice, we went back to that farm. It was hard going but we got there. Farmer Williams remembered us. He took us in for a bacon sandwich and a pot of tea.

He says, 'Now what brings you up here again?'

I says, 'Have you got any potatoes?'

He says, 'You know I can't sell them to you.'

'Who's to know? It'll be in yer outer – nobody will know. I'll give you four pound a ton.'

He opened up his eyes cause all he could get off the government was about five and twenty bob a ton.

'How many do you want then?'

'Four ton of reds.'

'Hmmmm. How you going to get the lorry down to the barn in the snow?'

'Don't you worry, she'll go down there.'

Down at the barn he had the German prisoners of war who was still working for him load up our lorry and off we went.

I must have had fifty ton of potatoes off that farmer at the finish. I sold them to chip shops in London for fifteen pounds a ton and they was glad to pay it. I carried on till I had a close shave. I come home one day and Mary was agitated.

She says to me, 'You been round the yard?'

'Yeah, I just dropped three ton of potatoes there.'

'Oh,' she says, 'for Christ sakes get rid of them. The inspector's been here.'

'What inspector?'

'The Ministry of Food. He's coming back at four o'clock.'

There was six tons of potatoes in the yard. I went straight round to see a greengrocer.

'Can you do with a six ton of potatoes?'

'That's a lot of potatoes.'

'Can you do with them – cheap!'

'Yeah, alright. Where do I collect them?'

'You don't have to collect them. I'll bring them round.'

Cocker and me sweated like hell to get them all out of the yard and into his shop by four o'clock. We had to make three journeys.

At four o'clock the inspector turned up at our house.

He says, 'Mr Day, are you handling potatoes without a permit?'

I says, 'What do you mean? I'm a bloody builder, what would I be doing with potatoes?'

'Well, have you got a lorry with a green tilt?'

'Yeah.'

'We have information that this green lorry is carting potatoes round.'

I says, 'You've got me mixed up with the furniture bloke in Bedford Road. He's got a lorry exactly the same as mine. You'll see it outside his house now, I expect.'

I knew they wouldn't find anything on him.

'Whoever told you must have the needle to me,' I says, ''cause I don't dabble in potatoes. I'm a builder as you can see. That's all me scaffling and tackle out there in the garden. That's all I cart round.'

Off he went and I heard no more about it. Me old brain saved the day – if I had been caught they would have put me in the bleeding Tower of London.

V

I reckon it was three months past Christmas when I happened to be passing the nick at Fortis Green. I thought to meself, 'I will pop in and see about that purse.' The same bloke was at the counter.

I says, 'Here, I found a purse just before Christmas, did anybody claim it?'

'What's yer name?'

'Day.'

'What's yer address?'

'Leicester Road.'

'Hang on a minute, mate.'

He got this big, thick book out and looked in it.

'No, nobody claimed it.'

He went and got the purse and put it on the counter.

'Shall I put it in the police fund?' he says.

'No you bleeding well won't,' I says. 'I'm good enough to bring it in and I'm good enough to take it out again!'

He says, 'You miserable sod. People generally give it to the police.'

I took the purse home and thought to meself, 'Well, honesty paid out that time, didn't it?'

There weren't much honesty in the ARP. We was supposed to give in anything we found at the bomb sites to the council depot back at our station, but we all helped ourselves rather than let that lot have it. All we thought about when we got to a bomb site was could we get anything for our wives and kids? If we seen food or clothing we picked it up, but we didn't take notice of much else. I took home tins of this and packets of that. All I wanted in that war was to know that there was plenty of food for me family.

After the bombs dropped we usually found several people alive down in the cellars of their houses. One day I dragged out an old boy in Hornsey Road. His house was all smashed up and flattened to the ground.

As I was foreman of the gang he says to me, 'Mate, there's a safe under there. Is there any chance you can get it out? You can have all the furniture – anything what you want you can have – but I must have that safe.'

So I says to the hounds, 'See if you can get it out.'

We got the safe out. Whether it was really his I don't know, but he quickly loaded it onto a barrow and wheeled it away.

There was lots of different sorts of bombs and then the Germans sent the doodle bug. It was a flying bomb that glided in and then dropped when the fuel ran out. The first time I seen one I was standing on our doorstep.

I hollered out, 'Look, Mary, there's a plane on fire here.'

It was going along more or less rooftop high – I can see it now – with a big flame coming out the back. Then the noise stopped, the light went out and all of a sudden – bang. Once after a doodle bug raid I carried half of a woman down from a roof. She had got blown out of the house and was wrapped round a chimney stack. I carried her down the ladder and put her in a dustbin. We all got used to this kind of thing and, at the finish, took no notice of it. The worst night was the night the German bombers flattened Hackney.

At Hackney the shelters was underground, under the road and the pavements. They held a lot of people cause Hackney was a populated district with lots of blocks of flats. When we got there after the raid the first thing I seen was a backbone sticking out the ground, no head on it. Then I seen another and another. It was terrible – all their heads was off. It weren't just one shelter but a mile of shelters and practically all of them inside was dead. The bombs dropped right on top of the shelters and the walls come in and squashed the poor buggers. Hundreds died down there.

The flats at Hackney was all buckled and very, very dangerous. The first thing we did was rescue the people trapped inside. Then we put the dead people from the shelters in dustbins and took them to the morgue. We must have picked up hundreds that day, mostly women and elderly people. They near enough evacuated all the children from Hackney so luckily all the kiddies was in the country. But their families was dead.

If you went to the council they would send yer kids away – with their mother if they was very young. But Mary had decided to stay in London where I could take care of her and the gels. One of me gang was a Welshman and he was a lovely boy. We was talking one day.

I says to him, 'I'm pretty scared about me family, them being at home on their bleeding own.'

He says, 'Why don't you send them down to my place, down with me mum and dad?'

I says, 'Where's that?'

'North Wales.'

'Oh,' I says, 'I don't know, I'll ask me wife, see if she wants to go.'

Things was getting very, very bad with bombing every bloody day and night so I put it to Mary.

'What do you think?' she says.

'Well, it's up to you.'

Anyway, she made up her mind and went. I took them to the station to see them off and when she got to Wales there was people to meet her. But it never worked out. The family was always talking in Welsh and Mary couldn't understand what they was talking about. She thought they was talking about her and she didn't like it so she come back. She was only gone for six weeks.

VI

About two years after the start of the war I got a letter telling me to go to the recruiting office at Burnt Oak. I went over.

I says to them, 'I'm a conscientious objector. I don't want to go in the Army.'

So they sent me away. A few months later I got another letter. Mary read it out for me.

'It says you have to go to a tribunal, Sid,' she says.

Off I went to Burnt Oak again. They took me into this

room that was just like a court and put me in the witness
box. There was a bloke and a couple of old tarts behind the
bench. I took the oath.

The bloke says, 'Do you have any objection to firing the
King's arms.'

'No,' I says. I weren't sure what he was on about.

'You're not a conscientious objector then.'

A few days later I was posted into the Army.

I felt very sore when I left Mary and the two gels. It was a
toss up whether I deserted or went. It was terrible leaving
me family there with all the bombing and not knowing if I
was going to come back and see them again. It was in the
back of me mind all the time. It was really terrible.

There was a lorry waiting at Salisbury to pick us all up
from the train and take us to the barracks and training ground
at Larkhill – near the place where them big stones are. When
we got there, cor blimey, it was the end of the world. I was
out in no man's land. They give us all our kit – a uniform, a
rifle and all that. Then we got shown how to clean our guns
and was sent to the billet to clean them. There was about
forty of us seeing to our guns when one silly sod pulled his
trigger. A bullet shot out and went round the billet, ricochet-
ing off the walls. It made a hell of a row. We dived under
our beds – it was a wonder nobody got killed. The stores
must have made a mistake dishing out a loaded gun, but we
thought we better keep quiet about it in case we got into
trouble.

The next day we done a bit of exercise – a two-mile
walk just to break us in. As soon as I got a chance I phoned
Mary to tell her I was alright, that I had landed. She started
crying.

She says, 'Shirley's got the bloody measles.'

When I put the telephone down I thought to meself,

'Hmm, what can I do?' I made an application to see the CO and I went to see him.

I says, 'I just come in yesterday and me daughter's got the measles. I would like to be with me wife and her whilst she's ill.'

'Got the measles eh?' he says.

'Yeah – the measles.'

'Alright, I'll give you twenty-four hours' leave.'

That afternoon I was on the train. I'm about the only one who went in the British Army and weren't in there five minutes before he was back on the train home.

The first few weeks of our training we went out on route marches and Gawd knows what else. It was hard, specially when they got us out of bed at about half two in the morning on mock invasion. We got trained to do everything to see what we was best at. One afternoon it was dispatch riding on motorbikes. I was a bit used to anything mechanical, so when it was my turn to ride the bike, up I went and stood on the saddle as I went round.

The sergeant was a bruiser with a big mouth, a right know-all.

He hollers out, 'Day, come back here! Where do you think you are?'

'I'm in the British Army,' I says.

'Don't let me ever see you do that again unless you got orders to do it,' he says.

I was glad when they told me I was going to be a driver and allocated me a lorry and a gun. I had to drive the lorry with a five-point-five gun behind it. The total weight was twenty-seven tons. We did lots of training, practising going down hills with the lorries near enough standing up on end. We had to put them in low reduction gear. The bloke would say, 'Take yer feet away from all the pedals and just let them go on their own.' We would go down the hill, hardly moving.

Some of the officers was bleeding hounds. I knew one of them who was a fruit merchant from Camden Town. He had been in the Army a long time and he had a lieutenant's pip. When we went out on parade we had to try to get what they called 'the stick'. If you got the stick then you never done yer guard duty. You had to have the cleanest, smartest uniform and yer gun had to be so nice and clean that when the officer looked down the barrel he couldn't see a mark. They gave us two hours off in the afternoon to do that. For the first parade I spent me two hours working like a Trojan on me gun. I thought to meself, 'I bet I'll have the best gun here.' We all stood in line for inspection. The officer stopped next to me and looked down the barrel of me gun.

He says, 'What did you clean it with – sand?'

'No sir, oil.'

'I've never seen so much filth in me life.'

If the gun had been loaded I would have shot him. I thought to meself, 'What the bleeding hell have you got to do to get yer gun clean?' I never did get the stick and I didn't care after that.

I was on guard with me gun one evening and I was thinking about a story told by me brother, Bill. He joined up before the war with a chap name of Holmes, who we called Bonk Eye cause his eyes looked the wrong way – really bonk eyed he was. They got sent out to Germany. They put my Bill and this Bonk Eye on guard and Bonk Eye seen something moving.

He hollers out, 'Who's there?'

Then he shouts again, 'Who's there? Who's there?'

You had to shout out three times.

There was no answer so Bonk Eye fired. Something fell over – it was a goat. He killed it stone dead.

I heard someone coming towards me. It was this squirt of an officer.

I says, 'Evening, sir.'

He said nothing – he just walked towards me down the line of lorries and took the gun off of me and into the guard room. In training they tell you the last thing you should do is give away yer gun – you must never part with it. So back he come with the sergeant of the guard.

Sergeant says to me, 'Where's yer rifle, Day?'

I says, 'He took it.'

He says, 'Who's he?'

'Him, sir,' I says, pointing to the officer.

Then this little short-arsed sod turns round and says to me, 'What would you have done if I had been the enemy and I took yer gun away from you?'

'Same as what you'd do, run for me bleeding life,' I says.

Quick, march – up the guard room he took me and read me the riot act.

It cost eighteen pence from the barracks to Salisbury town. That was a lot of money for us. If we had enough money we got a bus to town and bought some fish and chips. One night I seen a bloke I knew – he come from Kentish Town. I remembered him as a barrow boy from years ago, long before the war.

When I seen him I says, 'Ain't you Ginger Amos?'

He says, 'Yeah, I am.'

'Ah,' I says, 'you know me then, Cabby Day.'

'Cor blimey, I wouldn't have known you, not in uniform.'

Anyway, I palled up with him and one night, at about six o'clock, we was walking round where the stones was stood.

I says to him, 'I don't know about you, I'm bleeding starving. We don't get nowhere near enough grub in here, do we?'

'Nah,' he says, 'I could eat a dead dog.'

'Let's creep round the cookhouse, see if there's anything going.'

We was not meant to go anywhere near the cookhouse, so round the back of the cookhouse we goes. There was a little window and it was on the jar.

I says, 'Give us a hoof up, Ginger.'

I scrabbled up and in through the window.

Ooooh – I couldn't believe me eyes when I got inside, benches and benches of loaves of bread. I got through the window and threw two loaves out – one for Ginger and one for me.

We started out over the common to the big stones. We would sit in a big circle there for our Army lectures. They once gave us a lecture on the stones, how they reckon they got there and how many there was and all that. But I weren't at all interested in the bleeding stones. I couldn't care less – they was only lumps of stone to me. As we walked there I noticed something in the grass.

I says to Ginger, 'Look – these are bleeding mushrooms.'

He says, 'They're not – they're too big.'

I picked one up, peeled it and tested it.

I says, 'Here you are – they peel!'

'Oh blimey, yes. They *are* mushrooms.'

So we sat and ate the raw mushrooms and dry bread under Stonehenge. They was beautiful.

VII

When I finished me training they put me on draft. At the
Draft Board the bloke says, 'You're a driver ain't you, Day?'

I says, 'Yeah.'

'Scotland. Seventy-ninth Scottish Horse.'

'Oh,' I thought to meself, 'Scotland – all them bleeding
miles away.' But you couldn't argue. Ginger and another
bloke I knew, a barber, was posted into the same regiment.
This barber was what we called an iron 'oof. Before we went
we had seven days' leave. When he come back his foot was
bandaged up like a football.

I says, 'What have you gone and done then?'

He says, 'I dropped the fender on me foot.'

I thought to meself, 'The bleeding idiot.' A fender was
bloody heavy.

I says, 'What you do that for?'

'I thought I might get me ticket,' he says, 'but all I got is a
visit to hospital.'

I laughed. He thought he would get his ticket and he near
lost his bleeding foot. Lots of blokes I heard of tried to hurt
theirselves to get their ticket out of the Army. I knew one
shot his trigger finger. He still never got out – he had to learn
to shoot with the other hand. In the war, ninety per cent
didn't want to be there. Everybody was skiving, trying to get
out of going in – or deserting. There was loads of trotters on
the loose.

The 79th Scottish Horse was stationed in a wood at
Tunbridge Wells in Kent so I didn't have to go to Scotland
straight away. Till the war broke out it was a private regiment

owned by the Tate and Lyle sugar people, but then the Army took it over. The regiment had never heard of lorries – they had only ever had horses. The Army sent them drivers like me cause they wanted to get them mechanised. The motors arrived at the barracks three or four days after I did. Ginger and the barber was posted into a different unit to me so I didn't see much of them after that.

The regiment uniform was the same as everyone else's in the Army, except the cap was navy blue bodiced with a red bobble on the top and a tartan tail. That was the parade cap – we had a forage cap for everyday. We all had a little silver regiment pin and the blokes in the band wore kilts on parade.

I sat round talking with the Scots blokes and they tried to teach me the bleeding Scots language, but I had no use for that. We all got on alright, though.

First night one of them says, 'Dayo – while we're stationed here we'll do some of yer guards and fatigues. Then, when we get back to Scotland, you'll do ours so we can go home.'

'Alright,' I says.

And that's how they worked it with me.

We got fair rations there and a decent dinner every day. I got friendly with a cook and he was short of money. I had a little bit saved and so I lent him half a crown a week. He would give it back to me on Friday, when he got paid, and borrow it again on Sunday or Monday. He also gave me food whenever I was going home for weekend leave. He might give me half a pound of butter, or a big lump of dripping, or a lump of bacon, or a few bars of chocolate. I had plenty of grub off him – whatever I wanted so long as I lent him the half crown a week.

It broke me heart being in the Army and away from me family, so if I could get home on the train I would. More

often than not it was unofficial. One Saturday at midday
I was waiting for the train to come into Tunbridge Wells
station when a bloke come up to me.

He says, 'What have you got in yer kit bag, mate?'

I says, 'Why, who wants to know?'

'I do.'

He was an inspector – a plainclothes Army man.

I says, 'Well, this is what I've got in here, mate, here it is.'
And I opened the bag and showed him the food the cook
had given me.

'Where did you get this from?'

'Well, a chap give it to me,' I says.

'Where you off to then?'

I says, 'Finchley, outside of London.'

He says, 'You married?'

'Yeah.'

'Got children?'

'Yeah, that's what this is for – me two children.'

'You haven't seen me,' he says. 'If anybody challenges you,
you haven't seen me – but be careful in the future.'

I could have got six months for that. It was a very narrow
escape from going into the glass house.

I got away every weekend I could. One Sunday I got back
about twelve o'clock at night. Everything was dark in the
woods – I couldn't see nothing. I thought to meself, 'Cor
blimey it's quiet. Where is everybody?' Then all of a sudden
I seen a little glow of light coming down through the woods.
This little glow got bigger and bigger till it got to me. It was
a dispatch rider on a motorbike. He stopped.

'Dayo?'

I says, 'Yeah.'

'Get on the back of this, hurry up. The regiment's gone.
They're waiting to sail off.'

I got on the back of his motorbike and away he went like a bleeding madman.

I think I was about the last one to get on the boat. It sailed for a long time and when we docked I thought to meself, 'Where are we – abroad?' We started manoeuvres. Me and the other drivers had to practise getting our lorries and guns from the beach into flat-bottomed barges. They showed us how to get the lorry on and how to get it off. It was difficult cause there was only about two inches spare either side.

We was there about a week on the boats with the Navy. The Navy blokes had big packets of baccy and hundreds of cigarettes. But we never had a Woodbine between the bleeding lot of us. They got everything in the Navy – they got rum issues, cigarette issues, baccy. In the Army we never got a bloody thing! Nobody ever told us anything either. There was no signs – nothing – and we didn't have a clue where we was. After a few days we found out it was the Isle of Wight. Oh dear, oh dear! I had already got someone to write a letter to Mary for me. I'd told her that I was abroad and I was only over in the Isle of Wight!

VIII

After me trip abroad the regiment was sent to Scotland. We piled into trucks, put the horses into horseboxes and made a huge convoy about a mile long. We set out from the camp at Tunbridge Wells and went through London. We pulled over for a while in the Old Kent Road. It was Sunday and they was all in the pubs. Not one bugger come over and said, 'Here you are, mate, have a pint or a fag.' It was a different story in Scotland. We was heading for Kirkintilloch not far from Glasgow and we stopped in a village. From out of the blue people come out with jugs of tea, scones, cakes and bread. There was only a few cottages there but I thought to meself, 'Cor blimey, what a difference between this lot and Londoners.'

At the barracks there was about thirty of us in each Nissen hut – me and all these Scots blokes. The Scots got drunk just about every night of the week. I weren't much of a drinker but I soon learned how to drink more when I got in with that lot. We went to bars of a night time. When you went inside you had to part the air, it was that full of smoke. There was plenty of hard drinking and no women allowed. When we got back at midnight they got the bagpipes out and started playing them in those bleeding tin huts. Oh, talk about a row – Gawd almighty.

We went training up in Inverness and I never been so cold in all me life. It was that cold they dished out rum rations. We all got out our billy cans and I put mine in front of the bloke dishing it out.

I says, 'Fill it up mate – fill it up.'

'There you are.'

He put quite a drop in it. I drunk it down and it was lovely. It made me nice and warm. I got on the back of the lorry and fell down in amongst the live shells. When I woke up in the morning I was absolutely stiff, perished. Drunk weren't the word for it – that rum knocked me right out.

During that training I met a Scots sergeant who knew a mate of mine. We was sitting round in a circle in a field having a smoke when I got talking to him.

'What do you do in civvy street?' I says.

'I'm a warder in a prison,' he says.

'Oh yes, which prison?'

'Dartmoor.'

'Oh,' I says. 'Did you ever come across a bloke called Lee – a short-arse bloke with a big head?'

This Lee got nicked for stealing from the church round our way. The rozzers knocked him senseless when they caught him and he was put away in Dartmoor.

'Well, yeah, Johnny Lee, I did know him. Matter of fact he got shot in a bit of a mutiny down there.'

'So that's what become of the old sod,' I thought to meself.

We was back in Kirkintilloch for Christmas Day. All the top brasses waited on us rookies for Christmas dinner. Basil Lyle, one of the officers, come round with a big white tin jug full of beer.

'Oi, Basil, over here. Fill us up,' I says.

'I'll give you "Basil",' he says.

We thought we was in heaven with all the free beer and good grub, specially having the top brasses serving us. We all got as drunk as lords.

After Christmas I went home as often as I could cause Mary was ill. She was scared and she hated being on her own without me. She hadn't really got over having a baby and then the bloody war breaking out the same day. When I had to go into the Army she just got worse and worse. So I done more travelling to and fro than anybody. Sometimes I would leave Scotland about two or three o'clock in the morning, get home, then go back straight away more or less. Once I was back on seven days' leave when I got pneumonia. I was so bad I couldn't get out of bed. When the seven days was up Mary let the Army know I was ill in bed. A major come round to the house. He knocked at the door.

'Mrs Day?'

'Yes,' says Mary.

'Is your husband home?'

'He's up in bed.'

The major come upstairs and looked at me.

'Report for duty tomorrow,' he says.

'No, he won't!' says Mary. 'He's got pneumonia. He'll die if he has to get out of that bed.'

Then she told him off good and proper. I thought to meself, 'Gawd, I'm in trouble,' but she was always a woman to speak her mind. It was a good few days before I could get up and go back.

I had been in Scotland about six months when things got worse at home. Mary wrote a letter and I got a bloke to read it out to me.

'They want to put yer children into care,' he says.

I says, 'Oh do they? They won't do nothing of the bleeding sort.'

Basil Lyle was the officer in charge. I went to see him and told him about it.

He says, 'Get back on duty and I'll send for you.'

I went back on duty and not long after the sergeant come round.

He says, 'Dayo, you're wanted in the office.' So I went back to Basil Lyle's office.

'I've confirmed your case with your wife,' he says. 'You can have fourteen days' compassionate leave.'

Basil was alright. Once he gave me a rollicking when we was on manoeuvres for lifting a big gun on me own. It was a five-point-five, bloody great big thing on two wheels.

'Don't let me catch you doing that again. You're a strong man but you're no good to us if you hurt yourself. It's a two- or three-handed job to move one of these guns.'

'Yes, sir,' I says.

When I got home I could see Mary was bad. She was always crying and she didn't want to do anything. She would say, 'Sid, I just can't do it.' She had no strength. I bathed the children and helped out all I could. She had pills and medicines from the doctor but they did no good. He had told the authorities about her and they had been round to see her and the children. There was no way I could stay in Scotland with her so ill.

When I got back from leave Basil Lyle sent for me again.

'Day,' he says, 'I sympathise. I've got the same trouble as you've got with my wife, but I'm an officer and I can't do much about it.'

'Yes, sir,' I says.

'Where's the nearest barracks to your home?'

I says, 'The nearest one I know of is at Mill Hill.'

'How far's Watford from your house?'

'Oh, about ten or fifteen miles.'

He says, 'That's not too bad is it?'

I says, 'No, sir.'

'Well, you go and look after your family. I'm going to post you to Watford.'

So I packed me gear up and off I went with me bags to Glasgow station. I waited there, watching all the short-arsed Scotsmen picking pockets, and then caught the train to Watford.

IX

Watford was a clearing station for the Army and there was blokes from lots of different regiments there. I took me bike nearly every night from Watford to me home in Finchley. One morning I was going back to the unit after a night's unofficial leave and I was waiting at Mill Hill roundabout for a lorry carting hay. It went by at six o'clock every morning and drove from Finchley right through to Watford. As he come round the bend I grabbed hold of the rope what was holding the hay on to let him drag me right into Watford as usual. This morning, though, me bleeding forage cap blew off. 'Oh dear,' I thought to meself. 'Well, sod the hat, I'll buy a new one when I get back to the barracks. I'll tell them I lost it.'

The lorry was doing about thirty mile an hour, fast enough to get me back in the unit at half past seven. But then we come to the roundabout and a policeman stopped the lorry.

He says to me, 'What are you hanging on that for?'

'To get back to me unit on time.'

'Where's yer unit?'

'Watford.'

'Oh,' he says. 'Where's yer hat? You're not properly dressed. What's yer regiment?'

'Seventy-ninth Scottish Horse.'

'Never heard of it.'

I says, 'Me hat blew off down the road.'

'Why didn't you stop and get it?'

'Well, I knew I wouldn't be able to get back to me unit in time if I let go of the lorry and pedalled back and picked it up. I would sooner buy a new one.'

He says, 'Got yer paybook with you?'

'No.'

'Well, I'm sorry, you'll have to come down the station.'

He thought I was a bleeding German so down the station I went. They phoned the unit and eventually a dispatch rider come down to pick me up. When I got back I had to tell them the whole story and I was put on a charge. Then I had to buy a new hat for three bob. I bought a spare badge 'n' all for one and sixpence cause you could always sell the badge for five bob in any pub. It was a pretty badge, a horse rearing up in solid silver.

Not long after, I was on cookhouse fatigues at three o'clock in the morning. I thought to meself, 'Oh sod it. I'll go home.' The next morning I was hauled up to see the major.

'Left, right, left, right, left, right.'

They tore me hat off as I come in and slung it on the floor.

'Stand to attention!'

'You were meant to be on cooking duty,' says the major.

'I didn't know, sir.'

'What do you mean you didn't know?'

'Nobody told me.'

'Your orders were posted up in your billet.'

'I can't read or write, sir.'

'Oh.' He thought for a moment.

'Well, we can arrange for you to take classes,' he says.

'I don't want to do it, sir. I can't do it – me brain just don't function.'

'Well,' he says, 'you speak well for a man who can't read or write.'

They couldn't charge me and instead they made one of the other blokes read out me orders every night.

I didn't give two hoots for being in the Army and I skived whenever I could. I don't know how I kept out of the glass house. I never really mixed with anybody at Watford. I was always going AWOL and I couldn't care less what happened. All I wanted was to get out. In the end I thought to meself, 'Right, if I do something wrong and they nick me I'll get maybe six months in prison and I'll be thrown out of the Army.' So early one morning I broke into a dress shop and was walking home with the clothes slung over me shoulder when I see a policeman. I was in me uniform.

'Morning,' he says.

'Morning, officer,' I says, and walked by.

If you had enough front you could get away with anything.

I never did get caught out so I had to stay in the Army. The worst part was that although I didn't mind being told what to do, I did mind doing things that was absolutely diabolical for mankind. What used to get on me nerves most was fatigues on Saturday and Sunday. One fatigue was in the officers' mess. When they cut the grass there was stalks sticking up out of the lawn – they called them soldiers. They would get a gang of grown men to go round pulling these stalks of grass out. That was me weekend, pulling soldiers out of the bleeding ground when I could have been at home with me wife and children. When I had to do that I would think to meself, 'They must think I am a bleeding imbecile with nothing better to do than pull out stalks of grass. I bet they are inside saying, "Look at him, the soppy sod," and getting a kick out of it.' I had a family and me own business to run at home and they was giving me a job picking grass. That is the sort of thing that dements you.

In Watford I had billet duties too, cleaning mostly, making the beds and washing it all up. I was very clean in the Army and out of the Army, as far as I was concerned. One morning a bloke with one pip up come in to inspect the billet – a big private house. I thought to meself, 'He'll find no fault with this.'

He couldn't find anything wrong till he put his hand up underneath the wash basin.

'Absolutely filthy!' he says.

Now what the bleeding hell did he want to go underneath the sink for? It was bound to come out dirty. You could never do right in the Army. They did that kind of thing to show that they was in authority, to try and crush you. They come from nothing most of them and they thought they was little bleeding tin gods.

X

After I had been at Watford for a while, I got the draft to go abroad. The authorities was talking about taking the children away from Mary again so there was no way I could go. I was determined that I weren't going to leave me wife and children and I thought to meself, 'I'll desert and take them with me if I have to.' I went to see the officer in charge but he wouldn't listen to me so I had to try something else. I took one of the bikes we used for getting round the billets and pedalled it twenty-eight miles from the barracks to the Army head-quarters in Curzon Street. That was where all the big brasses was. As I was riding I thought to meself, 'I'll get down there, I'll sort something out. They're not going to send me abroad – I don't want none of that lark.'

When I got there I seen a bloke in uniform standing on the steps of this big building.

I says to him, 'I want to see someone about special leave. Who do I see, mate?'

He says, 'I'm buggered if I know. Where you from?'

'Watford.'

'The best thing I can tell you is go in here, go right to the top floor and you'll see a plate with Colonel so and so on it.'

'Well,' I thought to meself, 'this is good. I can't even bleeding read, how am I going to do that?'

Anyway, up I went and I seen this brass plate. I thought,

'This must be it,' so I knocked on the door. A soldier come out and I told him why I was there.

He went back inside then come back.

'Come in,' he says.

I went in and there was a woman colonel sitting at the bench, somewhere about forty years of age. I explained to her what was happening.

I says, 'They put me on draft and me wife is very, very sick and she's got two little babies – the eldest is six and the youngest one is three.'

'Oh,' she says. 'Where have you come from and how did you get here?'

'I've biked it from Watford.'

'You biked it?'

'Yeah.'

'Well, my advice is to get on your bike and get back to Watford as fast as you can.'

So on the dirty tyke I goes back to Watford. I suppose I got back there about five o'clock and I was back in the billet when the bombardier come in.

'Day,' he says, 'in the office.'

I thought to meself, 'Oh, here's a rollicking.' I went in.

'You've been to Curzon Street, have you?'

'Yes, sir.'

'Whose permission did you have?'

'Nobody,' I says, 'but they're going to take me children away. I'm not in the Army for that. I'm not standing for that lark.'

'You're on draft are you?'

'Yes,' I says. 'I was on compassionate posting from Scotland but now I'm on draft.'

'Well, I don't know what we can do about this. I'll have to have time to think. Off you go.'

Off I goes, home on the old bike back to Finchley.

I got back at five minutes to eight, just in time for the eight o'clock parade. After the parade the bombardier sent for me.

'You got to go up and see the old man,' says the sergeant.

Up I went to see the bombardier.

He says, 'Day, you can take compassionate leave.'

'Thank you, sir.'

The trip to Curzon Street had worked and they had found out me case was genuine. You had to speak up for yerself in the Army, otherwise they would do any bleeding thing they liked to you.

While I was on compassionate leave I bumped into me old mate Curly Coward, the steeplejack. He told me he had a building job putting an extra eight feet on the chimneys of a factory making TNT in Somerset. It was so the flames couldn't be seen from the air.

'Can you come and help me, Sid?' he says.

'Well,' I says, 'I'm on compassionate leave and I'm supposed to stop at home.'

'What's the name of yer regiment?' he says.

'Seventy-ninth Scottish Horse.'

'Where was you stationed?'

'Watford, why?'

'Well, leave it to me.'

He wrote to the Army and told them he needed my help on the job and they give me a six months posting to do it.

The job was at Dunball, near Bridgwater. Mary and the gels come with me and we lived in a cottage. It was a hard job cause they kept the factory fires going and the flames come out above the chimneys as we built on top of them. We made asbestos boxes to keep the flames and heat inside while we built up. We had to use plenty of water to stop the concrete going off too quickly and we had to watch ourselves.

It was a dangerous job, but at least we was away from London and the bombing – at least I thought we was. One day a bomb was dropped not far from the factory. It landed in a field and killed a cow.

XI

When I got back from Dunball I was posted to West Hertford-shire Cricket Ground. It was a privileged job and it meant I was not far from me family. I had to take care of the place, roll the pitch out with a petrol roller and mark it out for cricket and football so that the officers could play. I was me own guvnor.

Every morning a sergeant used to bring about twenty or thirty soldiers to the ground for drill.

One day I says to him, 'It would be a good idea if we put a rope on this roller and let them pull it up and down for the exercise.'

'Good idea,' he says.

He set them to it. Those soldiers saved me the two gallons of petrol a week I got for that roller. I sold it to the dentist who lived in the great big house at the back of the ground.

Not long after I started there a coal man come to the ground.

He says to me, 'Got any whites for sale?'

'What d'you mean whites?' I didn't know what he meant.

He says, 'Cricket trousers.'

'Awwww,' I says, 'yeah, come in!'

I took him in the store where all the spare cricket gear was kept.

'Here they are,' I says.

'How much a pair?'

'Three bob a pair?'

'Yeah, alright. Can I have four?'

I sold him the bleeding lot at the finish. I sold him the stumps, the bats, the pads, the pullovers – the lot. Buggered if I know what he was going to do with them all.

I must have been at the cricket ground for two years, and in all that time the hounds maintained it. I would say to the sergeant who was in charge of them, so and so needs doing. 'Right,' he would say, 'I'll get them to do it.' I weren't supposed to go home but I went home unofficial every night practically. But one night I stayed on till the early hours of the morning cause I had something to do. At about two o'clock when everyone was asleep, I got over the fence, killed six of the dentist's chickens and took them home to me family.

One day the Captain come down the sports ground.

He says to me, 'What do you know about baseball?'

'Nothing, sir.'

'Oh – well, if I give you a plan of a baseball pitch, can you get it marked out so that the Americans can come and play baseball?'

'Yeah,' I says. 'There's enough blokes come down here so somebody must know how to go about it.'

He wrote out a plan and give it to me. Not long after, the sergeant arrived with his troops.

I says, 'The Yanks are coming here to play baseball.'

'Are they?' he says.

'Yeah. They need a baseball pitch marking out.'

'Oh,' he says, 'that's handy. I'll set the blokes onto it.'

The next day we had finished it all. The pitch was laid out, the pavilion all spick and span, the coal dump whitewashed on the front, the food ready. There was big hams, cakes, lots of beautiful grub, all laid out. Then the Yanks turned up. They was wearing lovely flying jackets and they had bloody great packets of cigarettes, two hundred in a packet. 'Cor bloody hang me,' I thought to meself. The Yanks had so many fags – they could give anybody two hundred fags and get another two hundred just like that. We never had the bleeding money to buy a packet of five, never mind two hundred.

The baseball game lasted for about two or three hours. While they was playing I went round the back of the pavilion and got in through the window. I daren't go through the front in case anybody see me. When I got inside I nicked one of them beautiful fur coats and hid it to take away later when it was all over. Then I seen the big bowl full of dripping on the table. I thought to meself, 'That'll be handy – that'll last a long while at home.' So I nicked the dripping too.

After the game and the tea there was lots of food left over.

I says to the sergeant, 'Blimey, I could do with two or three tins of that evaporated milk for me kiddies.'

He says, 'Fill yer bag – I ain't seen yer. Take what you want.'

So I helped me bleeding self, filled me kit bag to the top. On the dirty tyke and home I went. Mary was so happy she laughed her head off. It made her feel better to see plenty of food in the cupboard. Nobody ever mentioned the flying coat and later I sold it to me brother.

XII

The war ended. All over London there was huge street parties to celebrate. We had such a big bonfire in our street we burned right through the road. When the fire died down we all moved to the hall at the bottom of Leicester Road. There was tables laid out with paste sandwiches and jellies and all the kids was in little pointy hats waving Union Jacks.

My Alice and her family lived near us and they was there too. Alice's daughter, Vera, got up on the stage at the end of the hall and twiddled a little tune on the piano. Next on was Mary with our upstairs neighbour, Lil Baines. They was done up lovely in floral frocks, feather boas and little cocked hats. They sang 'My Old Man' and dilly dallied up and down the stage with Lil carrying a cock linnet in a cage, just like in the song.

I stayed at the cricket ground till we was all demobbed in January 1946. I was glad to get out and I didn't want to wait for their bleeding suit. I just got on me bike and pedalled away to get on with me life at last.

When I left the Army me record said I 'gave every satisfaction during me service with the colours'. They never knew I stole the petrol, nicked the chickens, robbed the Yanks and sold the cricket gear. I knew one more trick than a monkey. I had to see to it that me family never wanted for anything. That was all that ever counted with me.

Not long after the war ended I met Ginger Amos over in Camden Town. I hadn't seen him since we was both posted into the 79th Scottish Horse.

'Cabby,' he says, 'you're a lucky man. There was only eight of us returned on D-Day, the rest got bombed out.'

Sid now lives with his family in Dorset. After the war he continued to work as a builder before following his daughters to the West Country to live with Mary in Yeovil. He ran a newsagent's for many years and wheeled his wares around the town's hospital until retirement. After Mary died in 1990 he became a fixture at local car boot sales and enjoyed searching for bargains and making a bob or two. He even ran a tiny second-hand shop for a while, where he was noted for driving an extremely hard bargain.

Sid last saw Balmore Street sixty years ago, but it still exists, though his house and four others were demolished in 1971. Older locals still know it as 'Tiger Bay', and descendants of Sid's family live nearby.